EALDIC

INDEPENDENCE

the library
IN EAST AYRSHIRE

Scotland
is a collection of islands,
the biggest ones jammed together

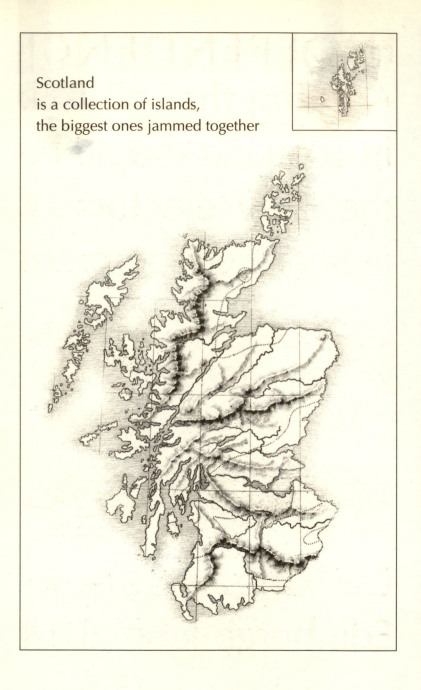

INDEPENDENCE

Arguing that all folk in Scotland should be the only electors of a Scots government

by Alasdair Gray

Canongate Books

Edinburgh 2014

Published in Great Britain in 2014
by Canongate Books Ltd,
14 High Street, Edinburgh EH1 1TE

www.canongate.tv

first edition

British Library Cataloguing-in-Publication Data
A catalogue record for this book is available on request
from the British Library.

ISBN 978 1 78211 169 6

Typeset in Optima by Cluny Sheeler and Canongate

Printed and bound in Great Britain by Clays Ltd, St Ives plc.

FOR ALL
INDEPENDENT
MINDS

TABLE OF

CONTENTS

Personal Prologue

THIS BOOK IS WRITTEN FOR SCOTS, by whom I mean anyone in Scotland who will vote in the September referendum to make Scotland a more or less independent nation. This leaves out many who feel thoroughly Scottish but can only vote in England, America or elsewhere. My argument is for changing a government, so I lump these with voteless children and criminals who cannot affect the result of the referendum. My definition cheerfully includes many who think themselves English but work here as hoteliers, farmers, administrators and directors of Scottish institutions; also those who live in Scotland because they have bought a pleasanter place here than they could get for the same money further south. My definition also includes a small but important group of Scots who mainly live and work elsewhere: great landowners like the Duke of ***** and Lady ***** of *****, who have homes and property in other nations but return to their ancestral home here to hold shooting parties and vote; also the seventy-one Scottish members of parliament whose working days are spent almost wholly in London so mostly live there. You may think this definition of a Scot too liberal or too narrow, but it embraces everyone north of the Tweed who has the right to vote, have a say in how Scotland is ruled, and therefore equally belongs to it. It should not matter how recently he or she arrived. The first folk here to call themselves Scots arrived from Ireland. There will be more about them when I refer to settlers and colonists.

My wife is not my severest critic (I am) but she is often severe. Though wanting an independent Scottish government as much as I do she calls this book a waste of time. Only a few of those who agree with the argument for Scots Home Rule announced on the cover may buy it (says she), none of those who disagree will, and folk without an opinion on the matter don't read books and don't vote. I have told her that before the general elections of 1992 and 1997 Canongate published my pamphlets called *Why Scots Should Rule Scotland*, and Scotland has since been presented with its own parliament, though a dependent one. She replies that my writing did not influence that, and may be wrong. The pamphlets were part of a public discussion, and if our debates, agreements and disagreements did not influence how North Britain is governed, then democracy here does not exist.

In 1951 a teacher in my secondary school called my essays on history "too personal", because when mentioning how those commanding armies and lawyers dealt with weaker folk I sometimes called the stronger lot selfish and unfair. The teacher told me that good, impersonal historians showed no preference for any social class in the people they described. But I believe impersons do not exist. All writers have a viewpoint, and only readers who thoroughly share it think it impersonal. Anyone trying to make a political point should start with an account of themselves, thus alerting readers with different prejudices to facts the debater may suppress or exaggerate. Here goes.

In 1934 I was born in an excellent housing scheme recently built for the kind of folk Victorians called lower middle-class and Marxists petit bourgeois. Our neighbours were a postman, nurse, local newsagent and tobacconist, and printer working for one of the national newspapers then published in Glasgow. My dad, born in 1897, was receiving a small government pension for a shrapnel wound received in World War I, for which he wore an abdominal truss. Between the two world wars he had worked a box-cutting machine in a factory. He was a Fabian Socialist of the George Bernard Shaw and Webb sort until the British government's pact with Hitler in 1938, when he joined the Communist Party, leaving it in 1939 when Stalin also signed a pact with Hitler. He and my mother were both literate and musical. My Scottish public schools (state funded, unlike what are called public schools in England) equipped me for a profession as my parents wished, so I had no sense of social inferiority. When writer in residence at Glasgow University I was amused when a lecturer in English from Oxford or Cambridge told me, "It is amazing that someone of your background knows as much about literature as *we* do." Many Scots friends thought my learning considerable; none thought it strange that I had it. Nor had I a sense of national inferiority. I agreed with my dad in supporting the Labour Party, whose government after 1945 brought social equality nearer to everyone in Britain, by using everyone's income tax to pay for national healthcare, further education and legal aid for those who could not afford these before. Both the Labour and Tory Parties seemed willing to turn the British Empire's former colonies into self-governing, democratic parts of a global Commonwealth. I imagined history as a story of continual progress to fairer forms of social life, with British Socialist Democracy an example to both the USSR and USA.

This view was so dear to me that on hearing that a Scottish nationalist party existed, I thought that an entertaining joke. I was sixteen at the time and had never read or been told that Irish and Scottish Home Rule had, with social welfare for all, been the declared aims of the Labour Party's founders in 1893. Only one thing inclined me to the SNP. My knowledge of geography was so bad that for years I had thought the populations of Scotland and England were roughly equal, so were equally represented in the London parliament. On hearing that both Scots and their MPs were a tenth of England's, I saw that in any conflict of interest between these lands Scots MPs would be so obviously outvoted that there would be no point in them voting against the majority. This seemed less important than the need to keep the Labour Party strong enough to stop the Tories undoing the degree of social equality it had gained through Westminster. Many readers will know why I stopped believing that.

Like my parents I am still a Socialist of the Robert Owen, William Morris, Bernard Shaw and Sidney Webb kind, but love Scottish political independence more, like Robert Burns, John Maclean and Hugh MacDiarmid. For most of my life I have been in show business, making pictures, novels, verses and dramas, which has perhaps made me too playful. With the help of friends my work has always earned me enough to live comfortably, so I have only an onlooker's experience of unpleasant work and politics. Being Glaswegian, my knowledge of the world outside that city is mostly got from books, films, conversations and shallow experiences of other places any visitor could acquire, but I believe my account of what I see as political corruption in Glasgow will be recognized as typical of other places by patriotic Islanders, Highlanders, Aberdonians and more.

One of my closest and most intelligent friends recently said in public that he would not vote in the coming referendum, because no resulting dominant party will challenge the capitalists ruling us. I still believe the vote can be a tool in choosing a government representing a majority of the electorate, but an almost useless tool in modern Britain and the USA where most of us can only choose between two parties managed by those whose wealth gives them nearly absolute power. That the Westminster parties have stopped representing many of us is shown by how few people in recent years still join them, and why the number of British non-voters has grown since the 1990s when Tony Blair announced that Labour was the party of the businessman. Everyone knew the Tory Party is that, so why vote for Tweedledum instead of Tweedledee? Leaders of both parties commit Britain's armed services to fight beside the USA in nations whose natural resources are treated as, not the business of natives living there, but our business. In Hollywood movies of the 1930s *Big Business* was sometimes shown to be selfishly greedy. Marxists called it Capitalism. It had caused a worldwide financial depression which both the economics of Keynes and what President Roosevelt called the New Deal planned to cure by spending taxpayers' money on public works. With the help of World War II these plans so succeeded that the USA, backed by Britain and some other states who think themselves democratic, has been fighting wars ever since, secretly or openly. The media told us these were being fought to save democracy. We now know they were fought to force the natural wealth of other continents into the international trading market the USA (with British support) dominated, and now shares with China. We now know this kind of trade and industry is poisoning the air, water and ground human life depends upon.

It will be hard for any nation to withdraw from what President Eisenhower in 1961 warned America against: *the military-industrial complex*. I now think the only resistance to that complex is an alliance of small nations co-operating to oppose the big military ones by pressing them to support the 1997 United Nations agreement, the Kyoto Protocol, to reduce carbon emissions. I hope an alliance of democracies could persuade millionaire politicians to take their weapons and armed forces out of other peoples' lands and waters. I believe the Scots parliament is about to gain more independence from the London one, but fear it may get it on terms that prevent independent action and use of our natural, national wealth. As Adam Smith made plain in more than one book, the true wealth of a nation is in well-employed people.

This book is not written merely to promote the Scottish National Party. While glad that it now dominates a Scottish parliament and is working to make it more independent, I am appalled by some things it has allowed, especially changes to the Scots legal system made by the Cabinet Secretary for Justice Kenny MacAskill. There will be a chapter about that. I will try to write entertaining criticism of many things, not all of them Scottish. Nor will I waste time by discussing Scottish identity, as vague a ghost as the identity of any other millions of people.

I acknowledge the help of five settlers here: Timothy Neat from Cornwall, Sharon Blackie from England, David Knowles from Wales, Angel Mullane and Feargal Dalton from Ireland. Scots of independent minds also helped, especially my research assistant Mary McCabe. This book will end on a note of restrained Utopian hope. Only the clinically depressed have no hope for the future. Those trying to discourage it under the guise of *realism* are what were once called *predeterminists*. Even Thomas Malthus, that prolific Church of England clergyman, hoped his *Essay on the Principle of Population* would keep Britain in a better state by stopping the wealthy improving the living conditions of their employees. Though writing of many bad states this should not be a gloomy book. Some of it will be gossipy, without offence to anyone's private life.

The coming chapters use passages from my other books, but few readers will have read or remembered them. The only exception is Professor Sidney Workman of Kirkcaldy College of Further Education, a critic who has always been out for my blood. Some chapters may seem like detours, especially the first, but all (I hope entertainingly) circle back to one idea.

You have been warned.

1: Britain from a Waiting Room

HAVING SIGNED A CONTRACT to write this volume for Canongate Books in 2012, I almost at once saw it a duty I postponed tackling. I hate duties, especially those I impose on myself. I therefore avoided keeping up to date with the political state of Scotland and Britain by only reading *The Times Literary Supplement* and magazines in my doctor's waiting room. I had an ailment which kept me visiting it steadily for two or three months.

I am fascinated by waiting-room reading matter. The doctor's surgery of my childhood had bound volumes of *Punch* cartoons, none later than World War I, though there were hints of it coming. A cartoon showed an officers' mess where a colonel asked a junior, "What, Captain so-and-so, do you see as the role of cavalry in modern warfare?" and was told, "I suppose, Sir, it will add tone to what would otherwise be a mere vulgar brawl." In another officers discussed an un-named foreign country. One said, "Yes, we'll have to fight them sooner or later. I only hope it isn't in the grouse shooting and salmon fishing season." In the aftermath of two world wars these amused and surprised me.

Later my favourite waiting-room reading became the American *National Geographic*, whose articles and pictures were always factual and entertaining. Yesterday in my doctor's surgery the only magazines with that name were very small, and seemed intended for children with a mental age of five. Other reading was mostly glossy fashion or style magazines, lavishly illustrated but cheap because mainly subsidized by adverts. Their many photographs of glamorous women attracted me more than I liked, because a married man of my age should have outgrown pornography. So I picked up *Focus*, a magazine for those interested in science and technology, and published by the BBC.

Like many who grew up before television I used to think the BBC a friendly institution. As well as the *Radio Times* it published *The Listener,* which printed radio broadcasts on literary, historical and scientific matters. In the 1950s it told me about discoveries of the Big Bang and continental drift. It had hardly any pictures, so in 1964 I was thrilled to see in it a reproduction of my best painting, which illustrated Anthony Burgess's review of a TV documentary about my art. *Focus*, unlike the long defunct *Listener*, has on every page bright photographs, computer visualizations and headlines that reduce the factual text to a series of sound bites. It is obviously for young folk interested in the future, not for specialists or older folk. It explains that **Neuroimmunology reveals how our own body can attack the brain**, and about a **New British project set to renew the search for an alien civilization** then asks **Could rising CO2 levels see Earth returned to the kind of climate not seen since the prehistoric era?** Suddenly a full-page advert caught my eye.

Central was a photograph of an aircraft that technically minded youths would know was one of the Unidentified Flying Objects developed by the USA. Radar could not detect them, so they were used to spy on the USSR when international agreements made that illegal. For decades the American air force fooled some observers into thinking they came from outer space. They are now called Stealth Bombers. Britain has them, for the Ministry of Defence placed this photograph under the slogan **We have the technology.** Beneath it I read: **The UK requires modern, battle-winning forces to defend its interests and to contribute to strengthening international peace and security. These forces increasingly depend on scientific and technological advances to maintain their ability to operate effectively: this means the provision of technologies of tremendous speed, power and capacity to deliver a decisive operational edge.**

We are The Ministry of Defence, Defence Engineering and Science Group.
Organization Description: Government Department.
The DESG is the team of thousands of engineers and scientists within the MoD.
DESG offers you many benefits including . . .

Here follows a description of secure, well-paid careers for smart young science graduates.

There was much food for thought in this. These graduates were not being invited to help defend Britain from invasion, but to *defend British interests abroad* – in other words, financial interests. The government of Britain once acquired an empire by doing that, and since then has not stopped fighting battles on the soil of poorer nations. That BBC advert was announcing that the UK government is still busy with the kind of arms race which led to two world wars. Yet it claims that the Ministry of Defence will **contribute to strengthening international peace and security**. That is how Big Brother now tells smart youngsters: "WAR IS PEACE! JOIN US! THE MONEY IS GOOD." Many will join. Compared with Welfare State students of pre-Thatcher days, the modern ones are a docile lot. Those without wealthy parents are heavily in debt when they graduate, so need well-paid jobs.

I picked up a journal called *All About History* which said on the cover, "Wellington won the war. Did Napoleon win history?" There was a final article about Edison and electrification. The rest were about warfare with the main article headed: **CONQUEST – EMPIRES GAINED BY THE SWORD. Subjugation and acquisition by force have been common since tribal times. We present a guide to conquests both ancient and modern.** The only women shown in it are a phalanx of black-robed Syrian women with their faces exposed and carrying machine guns. Thomas Carlyle had a cruel streak which made him approve of slavery for black people, but I agree with his saying that what is usually called history is interruption of life maintained by the cultivation of food and the other arts of peace. I forget whether this magazine or *Focus* advertised an improvement on war and crime video games such as *Call of Duty*, the game most played by actual soldiers, and only second to

Grand Theft Auto (produced by a Scottish firm). The improvement would allow several friends to enjoy the same visual reality while behaving differently from each other in a combat situation. Good training for the young?

A friend who saw video footage recording US soldiers killing Iraqi civilians from aircraft tells me their conversation about this exciting and perfectly safe business was exactly like people playing combat games. I believe this is partly because such games will be part of the soldiers' training. Since World War I, psychologists investigating British and American troops in battle had found that only eight out of ten deliberately shot to kill. Usually they just fired their weapons in the general direction of the enemy. This means that, despite the greater number of murders in countries where big business stops governments banning the free sale of firearms, the majority of folk have an instinctive distaste for killing others. I am also told that heads of our armed forces are now deliberately training their troops to overcome that distaste. Combat games must be part of that training. No wonder Julian Assange is being driven from one country to another for publicizing facts which our governments do not want us to know. I am glad a Norwegian MP nominated him for a Nobel Peace Prize, sorry it has not been awarded to him. I am glad Scottish students chose Edward Snowden as Rector of Glasgow University, though the USA government would like him extradited to one of their jails for questioning, for he too publicized facts that the bosses of the belligerent Western democracies want to keep secret.

I took refuge in the magazines with pictures of women illustrating adverts and articles about clothes, jewellery, cosmetics and food. They mildly excited me by constantly suggesting women want sexual fun. Under a picture of an excitingly dressed blonde *Style* magazine announced:

NAUGHTY!
THE OUTFITS, THE GLITTER, THE GAMES, THE BOOZE:
How To Have The Best Time At A Party
WOMEN IN THE KNOW: Let's All Move To Cheshire
BREAK OUT THE GLOWSTICKS:
Christmas Day, Raver Style

Marie Claire's cover says:

HOT MEN, SEXY ACCENTS!
The Europeans Revving Up the UK Dating Scene.
FIT AND FABULOUS!
Busy women's amazing body secrets.
BEACH BODY READY!
New quick fix ways to tan, buff and glow.

These magazines have articles about highly paid, visually alluring women, some emphatically married with children and good houses in pleasant districts. One has advice for those with too little time to properly adjust their make-up between leaving work and arriving at a party or dinner. It says "most of us" have several portable cosmetic cases (here called *palettes*) "because single ones usually lack items we find essential, or have used up". The solution is to buy an empty palette (available at a given price from a named shop) and fill it with just the cosmetics we need for that party or dinner. Since most readers cannot afford to buy such accessories as Prada handbags "surprisingly cheap at £450", such magazines are mainly invitations to daydream, though they must make poorer readers also feel inadequate.

British GQ is a similar fashion magazine intended for men. It has as many pictures of women, but they wear less, because women desire the clothes and appearance of the models in their magazines, but men desire their bodies. GQ articles never refer to marriage and home, and deal more obviously with money and politics. The cover shows a stunning blonde wearing nothing visible but an earring, and announces that inside we'll be told why **ELVIS LIVES!** and why **REAL MEN DON'T WEAR SHORTS**, and **HOW TO STAY SHARP AND COOL THIS SUMMER**, and also **(EXCLUSIVE) WHY GREED IS STILL GOOD by Michael Wolff**. In the 1987 film Wall Street, the central character yells, "Greed is good!" to a roomful of cheering shareholders. He is a company director who acquires wealth through buying productive companies, removing their saleable assets then closing them. He is cheated by a young protégé with a conscience who brings in a richer asset-stripper. The film's moral is spoken by a minor character who tells the young man to "Get a job where you *make* something" – by which he means essential manufactured goods, not just money.

Michael Wolff's GQ article is headed **YOU ARE WHAT YOU MAKE**, by which he means nothing but money. His sub-heading says: **The Eighties changed the way the rich get richer. Now, despite financial apocalypse, we still have an appetite for incredible wealth – and it has become insatiable.** He does not say widespread appetites for incredible wealth can cause only frustration for a large majority, because he says that for some people it will always be possible. He has a full-page photograph of a well-dressed handsome hunk of a man surrounded by eager reporters, for he is on the way to jail. It is captioned: **Michael Milken made, in a year, as much as $500 million. This made him much closer to folk hero than criminal.**

Yes, we have always enjoyed stories about highwaymen, pirates and successful train robbers. How many have wanted to become one of them? Do many fantasize about being fraudsters and pension-fund robbers like a former director of the Guinness company and Robert Maxwell? I doubt it, but without admiring them folk in national and local governments emulate them, selling to each other and associates the public properties and organizations decried as the Welfare State. If less than half *GQ*'s readers are in these governments, the majority must also use it to foster fantastic daydreams alternating between frustration and disappointment. What a lot of imaginary living headlines invite us to do! On a *Times* supplement cover I read:

THE RISE OF THE £100,000 HOLIDAY
Yachts, private islands and a plane for your luggage: inside the wild world of the six-figure getaway.

One or two millionaires have started a company which now sells the kind of holidays they enjoy to people equally rich. This may stimulate some to become richer by working harder for promotion in banks or by juggling investments through the Stock Exchange, which Michael Wolff says is the one sure way of doing it. I cannot be the only visitor to NHS surgeries angered by so many magazines enthusiastically boosting incredible wealth. My doctor's waiting room has no information about Glasgow's ruling Labour Party, which is funding a Commonwealth Games event by shutting centres that help disabled people.

My doctor's surgery is too respectable for magazines that advertise the sexual adventures of the rich and famous, nowadays called *celebrities*, and which would be shortened to *slebs* if that did not resemble plebs. Pleb has recently been publicized as a curse word. Since style magazines have also articles about food they certainly promote gluttony, lust, pride, greed, jealousy and (in jealous folk like me) anger, all of which were once thought deadly sins. The only one missing is sloth, unless holidays costing £100,000 are opportunities for that. But the MoD advert for the United Kingdom Ministry of Defence quango disturbs me most, though I know the sale of weapons is the UK's biggest export industry. Many pension funds are invested in that. In 2003 the principal of Glasgow University was a trustee of the British senior academic fund whose monies were mainly invested in the British arms industry.

Monsieur Hulot's Holiday is a French film I enjoyed as a child. It has a gloomy radio broadcast which, according to the subtitle, asks, "Is there, upon the horizon, one ray of hope?" On my horizon the ray of hope is a Scottish government as separate from the United Kingdom war plans as New Zealand, Holland or Norway.

2: The Naming of Britain

In three hundred and thirty BC
when ships always tried to sail within sight of land
at the west exit from Earth's middle sea
don't go through was carved. That small strait led
to the Atlantic that keeps moving its bed,
drowning beaches twice between noon and noon
and twice uncovering them, pulled by the moon.

It was hard to sail by Atlantic coasts
without splitting keel on reef or running aground
but possible, as traders from Carthage found
who sailed out with bolts of cloth, returned with tin,
carved *don't go through* to keep competitors in
and stationed warships to make their command obeyed.
The galley of Pytheas slipped through that blockade.

He was a Greek when Greece had markets
on every Mediterranean shore,
and learned from neighbour-nations more techniques
than discussed in one language before.
Greeks thought all knowledge theirs to explore,
enlarge and record for their extrovert civilization,
a thought that drove Pytheas to Atlantic navigation.

His boat, moved by oars and one square sail
like those in which Vikings cruised to America,
found an archipelago. From a tribe there he took
a name for it used in a Greek geography book,
a name that Romans spelled Britannia,
but during and after the Roman occupation
Britain was never the name of a single nation.

Only Wales could claim the old British name
when Angles, Saxons, Danes and Norman French
conquered south Britain, fighting until they became
one kingdom, England, which they fought to subjugate
every adjacent state. Ireland was the first colony
of her empire over sea. She conquered Wales.
France and Scotland won free.

Scotland was free till King Jamie the Sixth got news
that he could inherit England's crown too
if he lived there, an offer he did not refuse.
Like many Scots he went down to London town where,
Britain's chief landlord now, he signed parliamentary acts
to make these islands one kingdom
despite contradictory facts.

England and Scotland's clergy held
different kinds of Protestant creed –
hating Papists was the one point on which they agreed,
while Catholic Ireland constantly rebelled
against English landlords who bloodily quelled
their attempts to reject the South British yoke.
How could a Scottish king unite such folk?

King James, with the force of English arms,
evicted Catholic owners of Ulster farms,
gave their land to Protestant Scots whose immigration
diluted the Catholic Irish population.
No more (thought James) could they trouble *his* nation.
Such oversea meddling brought again and again
more and worse centuries of political pain.

To gain an empire whose sun never set
the English explored, traded, fought and won
mastery of seas and vast sub-continents,
helped by Scots and Irish whose parliaments
were both in the past, but left such outsiders a say
in the British Empire, though the USA,
hating taxation by London, soon broke away.

To make folk think the British Isles were one
Britain's Postmaster General called Scotland N.B. –
North Britain – and Ireland W.B.,
until West British rebels on an Easter day
seized Dublin's main Post Office, raised a Tricolour flag,
so that England's first colony followed the USA
when all but six Irish counties broke away.

National empires end. Britain's did –
Russia's too. Commercial empires remain
promoting war with drug and weapon sales
while parliaments in Ulster, Scotland and Wales
cannot stop the London government
sending their troops to fight in distant lands
when America's chief war-businessman commands.

Ulster Protestants may be last to gladly claim
the old British name.
Britain is still the irregular archipelago
to which Pytheas came.

3: National Geology

SEA SHORES AND MOUNTAIN RANGES are the world's only lasting barriers, but human need or greed, desperation or curiosity have never been contained by these. Roughly half a million years ago thinking people left east Africa and spread all over the Earth. Unlike other animals we could adapt to lands and climates in every latitude without changing our bodies much. Instead we changed our minds, habits, tools, diets, clothes, houses and whole ways of life. Social adaptation did not wholly replace Darwinian adaptation. People grew fatter and paler in the north, leaner and darker in the south. Un-migratory Chinese evolved extra inches of gut to get more nourishment from the rice crop grown on east Asiatic plains watered by three rivers, which explains why China is still the largest, most peopled and most ancient nation. Another self-centred nation was made possible by successive layers of limestone, chalk and clay forming a saucer of land with Paris now in the middle. The Baltic Sea explains why such close neighbours as Norway, Sweden and Denmark have different governments though similar languages. Differences of landscape still separate Portugal from Spain, Austria from Germany, Belgium from Holland, Scotland from England. Unlike sea shores and mountain ranges, big rivers have usually united the nations in wide valleys where they flow. They united China, Egypt, the Indus valley and other rich lands where the earliest civilizations grew. The river as political frontier was created in the 19th century when law-givers in Berlin and Paris compelled children on their side of the Rhine to speak, read and write in German or French, where previously they had used a hybrid of both.

Centuries before the birth of Christ the geology of Greece contained a great many small nations all sharing the same language, because it had many offshore islands and a coastline (like Scotland) about twenty times the length of much bigger land masses it was so sub-divided by mountain ranges, isthmuses and peninsulae. Greece became home of many small city-states with a variety of political systems: monarchic, aristocratic, democratic and tyrannical. The Macedonian king Alexander welded these into a short-lived Euro-Asiatic Empire, which broke apart after his death. All the pieces were colonized soon after by the super city-state of Rome. Simple geology cannot explain Rome's Imperial success, though its position in the middle of Italy helped, because that was also near the centre of the Mediterranean and halfway between Europe and Africa. Only social history can explain how Rome's small kingdom got rid of its king, became a republic which made all Italy its citizens (though only those with homes in Rome could vote) then became an empire ruled by the commander of its armies.

A map of the British archipelago explains why Romans coming here divided it (like Gaul) into three parts, calling them Albion, Caledonia and Hibernia. Albion was the southern and biggest part of the mainland: woody and marshy except on the chalk downs, yet offering few natural barriers to the march of Roman legions. The tribes of Albion combined to repel the legions and were defeated. South Britain got planted over by Roman camps joined to each other by well-built roads, and to Londinium, Britain's first major city. The Roman Empire had a warfare economy. Like modern Britain and the USA it used armed forces to steal the natural resources of other lands. The Roman economy needed new supplies of slaves as much as our own needs oil. Augustus, the Empire's first commander in chief, fixed its limits by using the natural boundaries of the biggest nations Rome had conquered. For centuries only frontier wars were needed to keep Roman slave markets prospering. Lands around the Mediterranean were thus kept fairly peaceful. The poet Virgil celebrated this in his Latin epic *Aeneid*, which said his empire had brought history to a good end, as the Roman peace (*Pax Romana*) would last forever.

Many educated Romans mourned the end of their Republic where citizens like themselves had chosen the political chiefs. They said so in writings none tried to ban, because the emperors and their bureaucrats knew such ideas were as irrelevant as birdsong. The historian Tacitus put his criticism into the mouth of a Caledonian chief who had led Pictish tribes to exterminate a Roman legion. It was then common before battle for commanders to make speeches telling their troops what they would gain by victory, lose by defeat. Tacitus invented for Calgacus (the Pictish chief's Latinized name) a pre-battle speech that nobody he knew had ever heard or could have understood if they had, but the speech is not misleading. Calgacus is quoted as saying what all natives defending their homes from the *Pax Romana* knew: "They make a desert, call it peace, then enslave us."

The Romans decided that colonizing Hibernia was not worth the expense, maybe because too few of them wanted to settle in a damp island yielding poor crops. Colonizing Caledonia seemed practical at first, for it had some fertile plains that continued those of Albion. The geological difference above the northern border was not at once obvious. They extended forts and roads into Caledonia but met such difficulties that they decided it was cheaper to wall the whole place off. The tribes that repelled the legions were not braver than folk in other lands Rome had conquered, but they had more natural barriers on their side. These barriers, this geology, explain why England and Scotland at last became radically different nations. British historians have written as if the Romans had *civilized* their ancestors by giving them written laws, metal currency, good roads and stone buildings. This is because historians are as much excited by notions of warfare and conquest as subscribers to the *History Today* magazine I read in my doctor's waiting room.

Rome began pulling its legions out of Albion in 388 AD, leaving the South Britons helpless against marauding invaders, starting with Picts and Scots from beyond Hadrian's Wall. Perhaps unwisely those Britons invited help from North German pagans who had not lost their fighting skills under Roman imperialism.

The Caledonian invaders were driven back but more Anglo-Saxon pagans crossed the North Sea to fight and settle in what they called Angle Land. They were
so successful that British natives they did not enslave escaped west, to survive in Wales and Cornwall. The new invaders liked the wooded parts of South Britain which were like the original North German homeland they had left. Stone buildings reminded them of the legions they had fought with, so their homes and the halls of their kings were built with wood at first outside Roman towns whose names ended in Caster or Chester. There is a verse by an Anglo-Saxon poet who was fascinated by the Roman temple to Hygiea at Bath. It says the builders must have been giants, because common men could not handle stone like that.

The legions had brought Christianity to Britain after emperor Constantine made it an official Roman religion. Before they were pulled out, bishops from Albion attended a Synod of the Catholic Church in Arles, a French city now. But the Anglo-Saxons wiped out South British Christianity so completely that days of our week are now called after their gods: Wodensday, Thorsday, Friggsday.

From agriculture, pottery and well-cut clothes to ship-building and air flight, every useful art and science has been achieved peacefully, without deliberate bloodshed. Without bloodshed they would have spread, perhaps more slowly but taking deeper root, where they were not imposed by force. The same is true of great ideas. Jesus took the commandment "Thou shall not kill" (which Moses had only meant Jews to practise between themselves) and told all people to practise it, choosing to die rather than kill. That is why his teaching spread first among slaves, women, and others too weak to resist masculine domination. It is why the first Christians refused to be soldiers. When the Emperor Constantine made Christianity legal, Catholic theologians said God had established the Empire before the birth of Jesus so that Christianity would be spread by armed might where peaceful persuasion failed. Though Christianity brought to South Britain by the Romans was eradicated by the Anglo-Saxon pagans, it took root in Hibernia which the legions had never attacked.

In 400 AD the nine Irish kingdoms were chiefly pastoral, had no towns, but many monks in small cell clusters. They taught the gospel from Saint Jerome's Latin Bible and copied out pages, often decorating them with beautiful, intricate colour designs. In their own Gaelic speech they wrote some of Europe's earliest surviving vernacular poems. The warlike Irish kings left these monks in to promote their religion in peace. The Irish missionary Columba brought Christianity to the Scottish kingdom of Dalriada in 563 AD, thirty-four years before the Italian missionary Augustine brought it to the Anglo-Saxon kingdom of Kent. In those days Hadrian's Wall, though an artificial rather than natural barrier, still separated warring Pictish kingdoms in North Britain from equally belligerent ones in the South. Confusingly for us, the Irish in those days were called Scots, so Dalriada was called the Kingdom of the Scots. By the 9th century Dalriada, through alliances and conquests, had given the Scottish name to the whole of Pictland, as a similar process was uniting Anglo-Saxons of South Britain in what they finally agreed to call England.

These two nations had radically different cultures. Their separate governments lasted into the present day with a hiatus between 1707 and 1999.

This is worth discussing.

4: Anglo-Scots Differences

A RECENT POLITICIAN supported what is now called the United Kingdom by saying that the wish for an independent Scottish government derived from nostalgia, not geography. Patrick Geddes, that practical pioneer of sociology, disagreed, for he said that all national cultures grew from the grounds where they flourished.

A land of broad pastures and good crops soon builds market towns which serve the surrounding farmers, and also public houses. Here the locals meet, drink beer, share ideas and future plans, and such pubs (said Geddes) led to parliamentary government more than the Norman conquest could. But where land is rocky, with thin-soiled ground in glens and valleys, the main crop is oats. The main cultivators are peasants who produce too little surplus nourishment to survive a bad harvest without extreme thrift. For centuries such a nation is too poor to have big towns, and since poor people in general notoriously produce more children than richer ones, a surplus population keep leaving it for wealthier places. They also think long and hard about money, so have often produced financiers and economists. Geddes mentioned England as an example of the first nation, Scotland and Switzerland as examples of the second. The poverty of Scotland compared with lands further south explains why Scots had a widespread reputation for what they called thrift and others meanness, also why so many of them emigrated that there was a saying in medieval French that rats, mice and Scots could be found everywhere.

In 1365 Jean Froissart, historian of European chivalry, came to Scotland and was surprised by the bad manners of the peasants. If a knight on horseback rode over a field the man who worked it screamed and yelled at him to get off. Scottish landlords, even if they were knights, were more dependent on the yield of their poor fields than French and English landlords with bigger estates. Scots bosses had to live closer to their productive class, so did not casually damage means of livelihood. Scots peasants and servants might not live more freely than those in other lands, but they were used to speaking more freely than English and French peasants whose lords had every right, in custom and law, to ride roughshod, hunting and hawking over peasants' fields without let or hindrance. France even had a law named *The Right of Plunder*, which made it legal for the military rulers in hard times to take poultry, pigs, grain et cetera from the peasants without paying. English laws were less harsh to their labourers, but in rich lands the killing of disobedient peasants only reduced the income of their lords when it became a massacre. So in one way, the Scots social classes were more of a community than the English, especially after 1066.

Many English historians have given the Norman conquest as much good publicity as the Roman. Read Kipling's poem, 'The Anvil'.

England's on the anvil – hear the hammers ring –
Clanging from the Severn to the Tyne!
Never was a blacksmith like our Norman King –
England's being hammered,
> *hammered,*
>> *hammered into line!*

England's on the anvil! Heavy are the blows!
(But the work will be a marvel when it's done.)
Little bits of Kingdoms cannot stand against their foes.
England's being hammered,
> *hammered,*
>> *hammered into one!*

There shall be one people – it shall serve one Lord –
(Neither Priest nor Baron shall escape!)
It shall have one speech and law, soul and
strength and sword.
England's being hammered,
> *hammered,*
>> *hammered into shape!*

Kipling tells us that the Norman conquest prepared the Britain he knew to conquer a worldwide empire of its own. As historical fact his thudding verses are poor-quality mince. England was not "little bits of Kingdoms" before William the Waster, with more sadistic violence than later despots, forced the Anglo-Saxons into his Norman-French empire. (Hitler and Stalin were seldom present at the massacres they ordered.) For twenty years before William came, England had been ruled by Anglo-Saxon monarchs and main landlords, an assembly of whom chose English Harold as their king after Edward the Confessor died. Nine months later, Harold II had just expelled a Norwegian invasion in the north when William landed his army in the south and started using his favourite tactic: destroying homes and farms of civilians to make their king rush into battle with him when he was ready for battle and his enemy was not. Harold II, instead of pausing in London to refresh and enlarge his army, rushed down to fight at Hastings and died there. William, now England's military despot, did not then hammer it into one. He evicted Anglo-Saxon landowners, replaced them with officers of his own Norman-French army, and replaced English bishops and church leaders with Norman-French priests. For over two centuries England was ruled by overlords who despised the language of the natives. This began to change when the great landlords and their officers found it easier to hold onto their French estates with the help of English private soldiers, so started using words they both shared. Of course the officers talked with an accent different and (they felt) superior to that of their men. They still do.

After France managed to expel the last of the English troops, England remained a united kingdom. But what had united the diverse regions, languages and kingdoms of Scotland? A map shows the mainland is like a collection of big islands jammed together but almost coming apart, an appearance given by deep firths, sea lochs and land masses that really are islands. On the west coast are seven hundred and ninety of all sizes, over half of them inhabited when they belonged to the Gaelic-speaking kingdom of Dalriada, to which Argyll belonged, and had its centre in Dunadd. To the south of that was the kingdom of Strathclyde with Dumbarton Rock as its stronghold, a name meaning *Fort of the Britons*. Strathclyde occupied the Scottish south coast and spoke a form of Welsh because it had been the north part of Wales before the Anglo-Saxons cut that in two. On the east coast south of the Firth of Forth English was spoken because those districts had been conquered for a while by Northumbria when that had been the biggest Anglo-Saxon kingdom. That is why those above the Firth of Forth had called it the English Sea. Most of the east coast and Highlands above it belonged to those the Romans had called Picts, who had a settlement at Inverness. Their language has been forgotten, because none can now read inscriptions that they left. The extreme Scottish north is called Sutherland because it was once the most southern part of a Viking empire which also for a while occupied the Western Isles including Iona, where Columba founded his monastery, and where four centuries of Scottish kings had been buried.

What unified that diversity again and again was English aggression. William the Waster ordered a

Scots king to call him his overlord which the king avoided trouble by doing, but no Scots became William's subjects, and he enlarged their numbers by treating the Anglo-Saxons in Yorkshire so harshly that many escaped from him by settling north of the border. What kept them different from the English was an economy that needed different institutions. England had many civil wars between lords fighting over who should be king, and those who managed to keep the job were helped by a House of Commons which represented the towns and cities. For centuries Scotland had no big cities, very few towns, hardly any parliament, so her kings needed the clergy to support them and so gave the Catholic Church in Scotland more wealth and land than (proportionately speaking) it held in England. In England the Archbishop of Canterbury headed the Catholic Church, sometimes with a cardinal appointed by the Pope. Scottish bishops refused to let one be superior to the rest, declaring that their only overlord was the Pope himself. When the Catholic Church was split between Popes in Rome and Avignon, Scotland accepted the French one, England preferred the Italian. When King Edward, Hammer of the Scots, tried to make the northern kingdom part of his own as he had done with Wales, Scotland mainly won her freedom because a Scottish clergy gave almost their full support to William Wallace and Robert the Bruce. Yes, the Church in Scotland served its kings well.

Shakespeare, in his history play *Richard III*, gives this splendid speech about England to John of Gaunt.

This royal throne of kings, this sceptred isle,
This earth of majesty, this seat of Mars,
This other Eden, demi-paradise,
This fortress built by Nature for herself
Against infection and the hand of war,
This happy breed of men, this little world,
This precious stone set in the silver sea,
Which serves it in the office of a wall
Or as a moat defensive to a house,
Against the envy of less happier lands,
This blessed plot, this earth, this realm, this
      England.

He then goes on to regret that England

. . . is now bound in with shame,
With inky blots and rotten parchment bonds:
That England, that was wont to conquer others,
Hath made a shameful conquest of itself.

Folk who like the land of their birth must often sympathize with that sad conclusion. It reminds me of modern Scotland. But the earlier lines invoke a lost, peaceful, triumphant nation which was never England, Scotland or (I fear) any other land. Shakespeare wrote when his nation enjoyed nearly a century of security under the Tudor dynasty, which had only suffered one short civil war and an unsuccessful Scottish invasion, but the Catholic Church made the Stuart dynasty one of the most lasting in Europe, outliving the Plantagenets, Yorkists and Lancastrians. The difference between the two churches divided their national education systems.

When the English language was unified in the 14th century the first vernacular translation of the Bible was made by John Wycliffe, and preached in South Britain by worker-priests. England's king, lords and Commons blamed the 1381 Peasants' Revolt on that, so after imposing law and order they ruled that English universities should not admit sons of peasants. This reduced by half the students at Oxford and Cambridge, and the practice was maintained till halfway through the 20th century by simply maintaining high university entrance fees. Earlier in his reign Henry VIII had William Tyndale strangled and burned for writing a new, up-to-date Bible translation, and after making himself the Church of England's Pope in order to appoint an archbishop of his choice, allowed the clergy to read the new English Bible, but tried banning it to English commoners. In Scotland the reformed Church, as in most of Switzerland, turned Calvinist and abolished bishops. John Knox and other Scots reformers wanted *all* Scots to read the Bible, and declared there should be a school in every parish where the local minister taught the sons of farm labourers beside sons of their employers. He wanted smart lads from every social class to enter universities, and in Scotland the tuition fees were low compared with those of Oxbridge. This system was never as firmly established as Knox wanted, but it was widely aimed for, sometimes achieved locally, and Bible reading became so widespread that before 1870 the Scots had a far more literate working class than the English. When after long delays the Westminster parliament ruled that education should be made compulsory for all children below the age of twelve, MPs spoke of having adopted the "Scottish system".

A lower standard of living combined with a higher standard of education explains why so many Scottish emigrants have settled successfully abroad. It explains why the secretaries who helped Doctor Johnson make his Dictionary were mostly Scots, though he made a hobby of disliking Scotland. I expect it explains why in 1972 an Oxbridge-educated tutor in Glasgow University was surprised that I knew as much about literature as he, though I had been educated at an ordinary Glasgow secondary school.

The Anglo-Scots difference persists, explaining why Scotland's political parties, Trades Union Congress, PEN and the Youth Hostel Association never merged with their English counterparts. It also explains why English academics who accept American and Irish traditions mainly ignore that Scotland has one, though it runs from the days of William Dunbar and Robert Henryson to those of Tom Leonard and Jim Kelman. How the Scottish parliament abolished itself between 1707 and 1999 still needs to be understood, for if it is not there is no chance of creating a healthier one.

5: Crowned and Uncrowned Kings

BERNARD SHAW WROTE A 1930s COMEDY in which an American ambassador tells an English king that the USA has repudiated the Declaration of Independence, so is again part of the United Kingdom, but the king must now become an emperor because "a king may be good enough for this little island, but we want something grander". Obviously Washington will become capital of the new British-USA Empire. On a smaller political scale this happened in 1603 when Elizabeth I of England died and her throne was offered to James VI of Scotland. Before going south to sit on it one of his courtiers warned him, "The English down there call us all beggarly Scots." That drollest of monarchs replied, "Don't worry! I'll soon make them as beggarly as yourselves."

In England he certainly did his best, financing what became the most riotous court in English history by selling off royal forests and other properties and also selling titles. He added over twenty new peers to the House of Lords. Under Elizabeth I it had shrunk, because she felt so much safer with the old Lords she knew that when one died she did not replace him. James may thus have made friends with the Lords, but when he needed more money had to ask the House of Commons for it, and the Commons only gave it on conditions which Jamie disliked but accepted while grumbling about them very loudly. But he was too wise to try ruling England without it, unlike his son King Charles who tried hard to do that. The attempt cost him his head, though the civil war he lost began with a religious disagreement.

James VI had lived in a Scotland where Presbyterian ministers preached that in the eyes of God even kings were not superior to themselves. His tutor, George Buchanan, had written a History of Scotland indicating that the people of a country had every right to change an unjust, unsatisfactory king, and the Scots had often done so. As a matter of fact they had not – Buchanan's historical precedents were as mythical as tales of King Arthur – but the book, written in a Latin understood by all well-educated Europeans then, had widespread popularity with all who liked the Republican traditions of Rome and Greece. James banned that book. In England he had inherited an Episcopalian state church reformed by Henry VIII, so that the king was head of it, ruling through an archbishop and bishops he chose to appoint. Jamie tried to make Scotland Episcopalian too by appointing bishops there. In the North East they were accepted as heads of the church, but through most of lowland Scotland their presence was tolerated while most Presbyterians went on worshipping as usual.

That was unacceptable to Charles I. In Presbyterian churches prayers were led by ministers who felt themselves inspired by God, so could ask Him to open the king's eyes to the error of the king's ways, thus inciting revolt. To prevent this Charles commanded that Scottish religious services and prayers be read from Church of England prayer books. When tried in Edinburgh this provoked a riot. Scots lords and commoners signed an agreement with God (they called it a Covenant) to never worship Him with that book. Charles sent an army north to quell these Covenanters, but without the support of his London parliament it was defeated. Then war between parliament and the king broke out in England. In a decisive battle the Covenanters joined the parliament troops, led by Cromwell, to defeat King Charles. England's government was now, in fact, Cromwell's army. It tried him for treason to English laws, found him guilty, executed him *without consulting the Scots*, thus enraging most of them because he was a Scot, one of the Stuarts who had been kings of England for forty-six years but kings of Scotland for three centuries. His son had escaped to the northern kingdom, where he was crowned Charles II of all Great Britain while England had become a Commonwealth ruled by Cromwell. A new, enlarged Scottish army invaded England, intending to put him back on the London throne. What followed showed the Scots at their most disunited, which always happens when they try to take political control of England.

The army consisted of four factions: 1. Covenanters who wanted to make Charles II king of a Presbyterian Britain; 2. Non-Covenanters who thought their victory would create an Episcopalian Britain by alliance with the Church of England; 3. Those prepared to accept a kingless British Commonwealth if it were Puritan, as Cromwell and his army mostly were; 4. Those who cared little for religion but wanted Charles Stuart on the British throne under any arrangement. If enough English had supported this army it could have triumphed. Not surprisingly Cromwell's counter-attack smashed it. He went on to conquer Scotland while Charles II escaped to Holland. Cromwell's victories in both Ireland and Scotland were celebrated in an ode by Andrew Marvell which had these verses:

> *The Pict no shelter now shall find*
> *Within his parti-coloured mind;*
> *But from this valour sad*
> *Shrink underneath the plaid:*
> *Happy, if in the tufted brake,*
> *The English hunter him mistake,*
> *Nor lay his hounds in near*
> *The Caledonian deer.*

The tartan plaid was a Highland garment and Scotland's diverse party politics were most obvious in the Lowlands. The historian Trevor Roper blames Walter Scott for uniting these in a view of Scotland only convincing to people outside her, but Marvell clearly took the same view that Walter Scott promoted more successfully one hundred and seventy years later, that most Scots were mountaineers who wore tartan plaids. This national stereotype may be as false as thinking America a land of cowboys living in skyscrapers, but since foreigners and even some Americans accept that view, while seeing the Scots as a lot of mean quarrelsome bagpipers, we should see such stereotypes as facts to be tackled while rejecting them.

Protector Cromwell (as he was called) finally governed Britain successfully without parliament, where Charles I had failed. He split it between his generals, giving Scotland to General Monk, who ruled more fairly than most bosses appointed from London. When the Protector died the House of Lords and Commons met again at Westminster and by a large majority invited the exiled Charles II back to be crowned king of Britain again, but in London this time. It was done. Charles's main aim in life was to enjoy it as much as a king then could without bothering about politics. He believed that any British king who did that would arouse opposition too strong for him, so avoided positive actions. The 2nd Earl of Rochester wrote this mock epitaph and nailed it to Charles' bedroom door.

Here lies our Sovereign Lord the King,
Whose word no man relies on,
Who never said a foolish thing,
Nor ever did a wise one.

On seeing this Charles said, "It is very true; my doings are those of my ministers, but my sayings are my own."

But Charles II and his ministers agreed with Charles I and James VI and I that the religion of the Covenanters be abolished. In Scotland the troops were officered by an aristocracy who preferred an Episcopalian king and bishops to a rabble-rousing clergy. Under John Graham of Claverhouse, an excellent commander, they willingly set out to destroy resistance among peasants and tradespeople who chiefly lived in the western Lowlands. These held church services on open moorland rather than worship God in a church where the minister read prayers written by Archbishop Cranmer. Charles II (known as the Merry Monarch) was an atheist, but his younger brother James was a sincere Catholic who felt enough kinship with Episcopalians to hate Covenanters. To make life harder for them Charles sent James north as his viceroy. When Covenanters were discovered, they and their ministers were shot without inconvenient arrest, trial and condemnation, and beheading was the privilege of a few stiff-necked aristocrats. This made the Covenanters more generally popular but also more determined and violent than those who were not.

These *killing times* (as the Presbyterians called them) ended in 1685 with the death of Charles II, and the former Scottish viceroy being crowned King of England and therefore the Church of England's lawful head. England's bishops did not mind a Catholic king as their head as long as he did not appoint Catholics to important jobs. Unluckily for James VII of Scotland and II of England, he believed that was what a good Catholic must do, and to make it possible published a Declaration of Toleration, under which folk of every Christian faith could worship as they wished. The Church of England was South Britain's only public broadcasting service in those days. To become official it had to be read from every pulpit in the land. Nine bishops refused to do it. James arrested them on a charge of treason, provoking such huge public protests that he had to let them go. Then came 1688 when the daughter of James with her husband William of Orange and a Dutch army invaded South Britain, and marched on London among so many rejoicing English that James saw he was no longer a British king and was not just allowed to leave for France, but helped on his way by enemies who did not want to make him a royal martyr like his dad.

So Dutch William, a Presbyterian, was crowned head of England, Scotland and Ireland and the Church of England. Very few bishops resigned because of that. The rest agreed to continue as usual after a law was passed forbidding any more Catholics to become British monarchs. With the exception of Catholics all other forms of worship were now tolerated in England and Scotland, and the Scots Presbyterian Kirk legally established. When King William died Anne, daughter of James VII and II, was crowned Queen of Britain, so the Scots again had a Stuart on the throne. What could they complain about now? Their poverty, of course, and the richest ones complained about it most, as is usual everywhere. English merchants and investors were profiting by trade with colonies whose ports were closed to Scottish traders. This led to the biggest, most carefully planned, most disastrous of Scottish immigration schemes before the 19th-century Highland Clearances. It happened thus.

William Paterson became for several years Scotland's uncrowned king. A financial genius, he had persuaded the richest members of England's parliament to create the Bank of England. He now persuaded the same class of people in Scotland's parliament to use their money to establish a Scottish colony on the Isthmus of Panama. Maps showed this could be a convincing way for Scotland to trade with all the ports around both the Atlantic and Pacific. Scots landowners and merchants were so convinced that they invested all their surplus wealth in the scheme, as heartily as twenty years later the English invested in the South Sea Bubble. The Scots knew Paterson was certainly not out to mislead his own people. He led the colonists who sailed to Darién where two centuries later a French company began digging the Panama Canal. But the coast was a jungle and a fever trap. The nearest European settlements were Spanish, who blockaded the Scottish settlement. The Royal English Navy refused to defend it. The scheme foundered and Paterson returned, one of those who had not lost his life through fever.

Scottish independence took another hard knock. Queen Anne was a Stuart, so accepted as a Scottish monarch, but she had borne no children and was too old to have one. The only remaining extant Stuarts were Catholics under the protection of the French monarchy, and hardly any major English property owners wanted them back. The London parliament decided that no Catholic would ever again wear the British Crown, and without consulting the Scottish parliament, decided that on Queen Anne's death the Crown would pass to her nearest Protestant relation, who was a German Duchess of Hanover, or if she died first, her son. The Scots parliament decided this was something they would not accept outright, but negotiate about, and sent some of its members to London to do the negotiating. They did not send Paterson, but he was already in London and as one of the founders of the Bank of England, a useful middle man.

The negotiators returned with the proposal that the Scottish parliament abolish itself by joining Westminster, by adding 45 Scots MPs to 513 English and Welsh commoners, and 16 Scots lords to 190 in the House of Lords, and having all Scottish taxes going to Westminster. In return, Scotland would be allowed to keep its ancient laws and legal system, the Presbyterian church would become the established Chuch of Scotland and the Scottish parliament would receive an immediate cash payment of £398,085 and 10 shillings. This precise number exactly equalled the Scots investment in the failed Scottish trading company responsible for the Darien Scheme. This was not generous of England, since the English treasury would recover it by taxing Scotland. Nor did the Scots–English ratio of 45 to 513 correspond to the population of Scots to English. Cornwall had 45 MPs.

My friend Paul Scott, a former British diplomat, has said that centuries of diplomacy have taught English negotiators exactly how much to pay for agreements they want, and how much threat to enforce them. The London government also said that if the Scottish parliament refused these terms it would put a total embargo on all Scottish trade, even if they shared the same king. England then had coastal ports and factories in Asia, India, America and the Caribbean, and was still rich enough to be successfully fighting a war with France in Europe, where France was the richest nation. The threat of war with a disobedient

Scotland need not be mentioned because it was an obvious possibility.

During the long debate on the Union Treaty an English spy told his government that the Scots people were 50 to 1 against this treaty. The Scots parliament accepted it and were denounced by nearly all the Scottish clergy, protested against by nearly all local town councils, and there were riots against it in Edinburgh, Glasgow and Dumfries. So in 1707 the Speaker of the Scots parliament was too scared of rioters outside to announce it had abolished itself, so said it was adjourned. In 1999 when the next Scots parliament met in the Church of Scotland's Assembly Rooms in Edinburgh, it could claim to have reconvened.

For years after 1707 many on both sides of the border thought the Union a disaster. Only a tenth part of the London parliament was Scottish MPs: they could only influence it by voting for the party who most bribed them, in centuries when bribery was legal and expected; they mostly voted for what was called "the king's party", because George III could give many perquisites to his supporters, and though sometimes insane, interfered with parliamentary business when he was not, much to the annoyance of leading Whigs like Burke, Pitt and that proto-democrat John Wilkes who edited a magazine called The North Briton, to denounce Scottish influence. It blamed the Earl of Bute, a Scottish Prime Minister, for the American Declaration of Independence and loss of North Atlantic colonies. Robert Burns gave a Scottish view of the Union in a song.

Fareweel to a' our Scottish fame,
Fareweel our ancient glory;
Fareweel ev'n to the Scottish name,
Sae fam'd in martial story.
Now Sark rins over Solway sands,
An' Tweed rins to the ocean,
To mark where England's province stands –
Such a parcel of rogues in a nation!

What force or guile could not subdue,
Thro' many warlike ages,
Is wrought now by a coward few,
For hireling traitor's wages.
The English steel we could disdain,
Secure in valour's station;
But English gold has been our bane –
Such a parcel of rogues in a nation!

O would, ere I had seen the day
That Treason thus could sell us,
My auld grey head had lain in clay,
Wi' Bruce and loyal Wallace!
But, pith and power, till my last hour,
I'll mak this declaration;
We're bought and sold for English gold –
Such a parcel of rogues in a nation!

But certainly the Union made overseas trade easy for Scottish merchants. Protected by the Royal British Navy they acquired sugar, cotton and tobacco plantations in the Caribbean and southern states of America, working them with enslaved black people from Africa. Side by side with the English they got factories and tea plantations in India, the opium trade and a major bank in China. Their companies imported raw materials and luxury items from every continent while exporting back utensils and fabrics made in Scotland. Scottish soldiers left the land to fight for the expanding British Empire, because while the English kept their own name for South Britain, their parliament used for the Empire a more uniting adjective. Not all Scots soldiers fought willingly for this Empire, as I will explain later. But as the 18th century advanced and Scots prosperity grew, the absence of a Scottish parliament in Edinburgh and the remoteness of the British parliament in London gave the most enquiring minds in Scottish universities a sense of unrestricted freedom, hence that movement called the Scottish Enlightenment.

The Enlightenment throughout Europe took its name from a remark by the German philosopher Immanuel Kant, that problems could be investigated in a better light if examined without prejudices, by which he meant *religious* prejudices. The best Scots minds had already broken free of Hellfire Old Testament Presbyterianism. David Hume, widely thought the foremost of modern philosophers, had this in common with Doctor Johnson (who loathed him) that in youth both had been taught to fear that their natural wishes would damn their souls eternally to Hell. Hume escaped from that fear by finding nothing in himself that could outlive his body, and stopped fearing death because God would not eternally torture him after it. (Johnson thought that possible.) This enlightenment allowed Hutton's investigations of Scotland's geological strata to conclude that there was no evidence that the world ever had a beginning or would come to an end, and expanded to eternity a widely accepted biblical calculation that the universe was roughly three thousand years old and would end in a few lifetimes. Adam Smith's *Wealth of Nations* has dominated economic thinking ever since, though economists now distort it to mean bankers should overrule governments. In Glasgow University the pioneer physicist Professor Joseph Black helped James Watt toward his invention of the first efficient steam engine which led to a worldwide industrial revolution. The *Encyclopedia Britannica* was first published in Edinburgh, in three volumes between 1768 and 1771, by William Smellie (who also published the poems of Burns) and was published there until the 9th and most scholarly edition of 1875–89, after which the publishers moved to London, then to the USA, when Scotland, except in fields of medicine and science, was no longer Britain's main literary capital city. In his autobiography Edward Gibbon says Hume's *History of England* partly inspired him to write *The History of the Decline and Fall of the Roman Empire*, and prints in full a letter of congratulation from Hume when the first volume of that work appeared. It says that, had he not met Hume personally, *"such a performance from an Englishman in our age would have given me some surprise. You may smile at this sentiment, but it seems to me that your countrymen, for almost a whole generation, have given themselves up to barbarous and absurd faction* [by this Hume means party politics]*, and have totally neglected all polite letters. I no longer expected any valuable production to come from them . . . all men of letters in this place concur in their admiration of your work."*

This intellectual dominance of Scottish literature lasted till after the death of Walter Scott, because the main Liberal and Tory journals and book reviews were published in Edinburgh.

But Scotland was mainly free of party politics because her own politics were manipulated by one of her longest-lasting uncrowned kings, Henry Dundas, Solicitor General for Scotland, MP for Midlothian and Edinburgh, who for thirty years between 1775 and 1805 managed the whole political patronage of Scotland on London's behalf. The patronage system ensured that nobody could have a job with or under government unless appointed by a great landlord. Independent America and some middle-class voters in England had partly freed themselves from this system, which those who wanted democracy called Old Corruption. Even those who believed democracy was nothing but mob rule suspected a fairer political system was possible, if the property-owning classes were allowed to vote for MPs.

6: Old and New Corruption

DURING THE WARS WITH FRANCE that began with the French Revolution and ended with the despotism of Napoleon, many Britons still wanted parliamentary reform, which made the Westminster government nervous. It made criticism of it *sedition*, a punishable crime, banned Thomas Paine's book *Rights of Man*, jailed folk for passing it around and set up a network of spies. One of these listened in to conversations between the poets Wordsworth and Coleridge who were suspected of radical politics. Wordsworth later became so Conservative that he was put in charge of selling postage stamps in the Lake District, a sinecure which increased his small unearned income. Old Corruption flourished until the long delayed 1832 Reform Act. When denounced the parliamentary answer was, "Corruption is as notorious as the sun at noonday," meaning it must last as long as the sun. How could any government exist without it?

After the Victorian middle class got the vote in 1832 they set out to reduce corruption, not by paying MPs (who were expected to have private sources of income) but by paying good wages to civil servants, who were not expected to profit by private jobs. But civil servants then could openly belong to political parties and even start them. The Labour Party was founded by Socialist civil servants reaching agreements with the trade unions. The life expectancy of labourers in those days was less than fifty years, which was mainly caused by malnutrition and living in slums with a huge infant death rate. Malthusian economists argued that only a high working-class death rate could prevent overpopulation. The Labour Party did not believe healthy living conditions for all would destroy British prosperity. Its declared aim was public ownership of essential industry starting with the land, also Home Rule for Ireland and Scotland. Many in the Liberal Party shared these aims, so what was called the Lib–Lab Pact came about. Its most active members were Keir Hardie, a Scottish ex-coalminer elected to Westminster in 1892 as the Independent Labour Party MP for West Ham. And Robert Cunninghame Graham, Liberal MP for North West Lanarkshire, though an aristocrat descended from Robert the Bruce, was elected the first president of the Scottish Labour Party in 1888.

Before 1914 a majority of Irish MPs in the Commons so regretted the loss of their own parliament in 1801 that they wanted it back. They interrupted English parliamentary business so often in efforts to get it that they seemed about to succeed when the Great War started. The other MPs decided to wait till Britain had won before seriously discussing Irish Home Rule. In 1916 Dublin's General Post Office was occupied by a small armed body of Irish who raised the Republican flag and declared that Ireland now *was* independent. What they had hoped for and expected then took place. Instead of laying siege to the building until starvation forced surrender on the rebels, an English general ordered Dubliners in nearby houses (some with sons fighting for Britain in France) to be expelled, making room for big guns. The Post Office was shelled, the rebels surrendered and were shot. So in the first general election after the Great War the Irish elected a majority of Sinn Féin MPs who refused to go to Westminster, but reopened their own parliament in Dublin.

In the 1924 general election on the British mainland the Labour Party won a small parliamentary majority and its leader, Ramsay MacDonald, became Prime Minister. This came about partly through a surprising number of new MPs elected on Clydeside when (it was said) "the Clyde went red". This victory had been prepared by many left-wing associations: trade unions, the Independent Labour Party, Communists, musical and outdoor activity clubs, Socialist Sunday Schools (Protestant organizations) and the Catholic Socialist Society. These marched in thousands to cheer the new MPs leaving for London from Saint Enoch's Station, which has now been replaced by a huge shopping mall. In those days the entrance was reached by a long external ramp. The crowd assembled in Saint Enoch's Square and the departing MPs made speeches to them from the top of the ramp. My father was there and told me that Jimmy Maxton, MP for Bridgeton, got the biggest cheer when he announced, "When we return this station will be ours!" because nationalization of railways was Independent Labour Party policy. But there had to be World War II before that happened, and it did not last. Perhaps the most sensible thing said on that occasion was by Guy Aldred, an English anarchist who chose to live in Glasgow because he thought the people there more open to radical ideas. Aldred said the new Scottish MPs should stay in Scotland and form a government of their own as the Irish had done. He may have been right.

The new Labour government lasted less than a year, but its Minister of Health was John Wheatley, founder of the Catholic Socialist Society, and by great exertions he got what were called the Wheatley Acts passed, which enabled local governments to build good quality housing with the support of local and central government. The son of an Irish coalminer with a large family, like a majority of the Scottish working class he had grown up in slum conditions which he wanted replaced by something better. I am grateful to him as his struggle produced those excellent Glasgow housing schemes, Knightswood and Riddrie, in the last of which I was born. These were the earliest two Glasgow housing schemes and the best planned, with convenient shops, schools, public libraries, bowling greens and adjacent parklands with sports facilities. Homes in later schemes also had as many bedrooms, bathrooms and kitchens with hot and cold running water but were built more cheaply with fewer adjacent social amenities. Between the world wars that was the only Socialist measure the Labour Party achieved, though the party soon replaced the Liberals as the Tory Party's main opponent. It did not renounce Scottish Home Rule as an aim, but without Irish MPs in Westminster making a fuss about it the matter seemed less urgent. When the Wall Street Crash of 1929 produced a worldwide slump in trade and soaring unemployment, the Tory and parliamentary Labour Parties formed a National Government Coalition with Ramsay MacDonald as Prime Minister. Only a small group of the Independent Labour MPs stayed in opposition. MacDonald had once sounded as Socialist as them. When speaking for Britain when Prime Minister in the 1930s his most memorable words were, "We shall go on and on and on, and up and up and up." He was verging on senility and the Tories did not mind anyone who was not embarrassed laughing at him.

By that time the Scottish Labour MPs had so lost interest in Home Rule that in 1934 a Scottish National Party was founded with that aim only. It was formed by Socialists who no longer expected action from the Labour Party, Communists who refused to let Moscow dictate to them, writers and journalists of whom the poet Hugh MacDiarmid was greatest, and a few aristocrats, with the former Scottish Labour Party leader Cunninghame Graham the notable first president. After six years as an MP in the Commons he had left it saying nobody could work long there without being dirtied, by which I think he meant compromised. He also said an Edinburgh parliament would probably be corrupt too, but might have fewer opportunities.

The Horse's Mouth is a great novel published a year after the end of World War II. In it the artist hero says, "The only good government is a bad government in a fright." The author Joyce Cary was thinking of the Labour–Tory–Liberal National Coalition government which led

Britain through the war. Faced by a European mainland wholly ruled by a Fascist alliance, it had taken control of British industry, frozen all company profits, frozen wages for everyone through deals with the trade unions, introduced food rationing and universal conscription, not just into the armed forces but into coalmining and arms manufacture: in fact it had nationalized everything the Labour Party had proposed in 1892 with the exception of land and banks. By 1940 the only unemployed in Britain were elderly and retired, and the wealthiest among these had most of their big houses requisitioned for use as hospitals or new government offices the war effort needed. Boyd Orr was appointed Minister of Health. A farmer's son who trained as a doctor in Glasgow University, he was horrified by the shorter lives of those housed in the slums. He blamed it mainly on hunger and malnutrition so worked all his life to cure that, first starting a research farm near Aberdeen to show farmers how to get a higher yield from their land, then helping to create the Milk Marketing Board and persuading the government to provide children from all parents except the richest with regular supplies of milk through their schools. During the war he introduced health inspection through the schools, and had children whose health needed it dosed with cod-liver oil and orange juice. When the war ended, British children were the healthiest generation that had existed since public health records had been instituted at the start of the 20th century.

Not surprising then, that the Labour Party overwhelmingly won the first general election after the war. It promised to make permanent the public ownership of transport, mining, steel production and health services, while agreeing to trade union demands for better working conditions: forty-four paid hours of work per week, double pay for voluntary overtime with tea breaks and regular holidays. This founded the British Welfare State, not yet wholly disbanded. Conservatives grumbled against it but not very hard. The Labour government bought their shares in nationalized industries for a price which amply compensated them, and before the war started their unearned income from these shares had shrunk to very little. Also many of their leaders had fought in World War I, and knew that the British government's promise to give the survivors "a land fit for heroes to live in" had been false, so wanted to keep some of the promises they had made during the recent war. So for at least twenty years the Conservatives did not begin to dismantle this Welfare State, and in the 1960s the Tory Prime Minister, Harold Macmillan, told the British, "You've never had it so good."

Meanwhile in Scotland the Scottish National Party was starting to take root and grow, more to the annoyance of Labour leaders than Conservatives, because the Conservatives' strongest base had always been England, while its opposition had been strongest in Scotland, which was mainly Liberal throughout the 19th century and mainly Labour throughout the 20th. The Scottish Labour Party had no wish to take over the Scottish National Party vote by returning to the original policy of its founders, Keir Hardie and Cunninghame Graham. In Westminster between the world wars they had helped to rule the biggest empire the world had ever known and even after the empire collapsed, the United Kingdom felt it was one of the big boys, being in the Security Council of the United Nations and having nuclear missiles beside the USA, USSR and China. When the British Prime Minister Cameron visited China recently, the Chinese equivalent of *Pravda*, a newspaper voicing government views, had an article saying that Britain had a number of good football teams but was otherwise an unimportant European nation. The writer was ignoring the UK's close military and financial links with the USA. Like China and the USA it also has enough nuclear submarines and missiles to destroy human life on Earth *and* a number of good football teams. Of course Scots Labour MPs did not wish to leave Westminster, the command centre of so powerful a nation, which has also been called "the best club in the world". One of them told a friend of mine, "No matter what your interest is – fishing, philately, art or Chinese porcelain – you can always find someone else in the Commons to share it with."

Alas, this has led to the return of Old Corruption.

Perhaps it never went away but for many years it was inconspicuous. Stanley Baldwin, a highly Conservative British Prime Minister between the wars, caused annoyance among his supporters by suggesting wrong business practices had caused the economic depression. In the post-war Labour government a Cabinet minister had to return to his old job of selling railway tickets because of a newspaper story telling the nation that he had accepted an expensive overcoat from one of those who were then reviled as *middle men*, and since Thatcher's time have been praised as *entrepreneurs*. In the last year or two of his government Harold Wilson was criticized in the Commons because his private secretary had been enriched by the purchase of properties whose value had been increased in ways she must have learned by working for him. Both Tory and Labour MPs criticized him for employing her. He answered them by giving her a title in the next Honours list. This shocked a few Labour MPs but pleased the Tories. I heard on the BBC news a prominent Tory almost chortling as he said, "Say what you like about that, but it's certainly a thoroughly 18th-century response." By 18th-century of course he meant *corrupt*.

Which brings us to what followed the discovery of Britain's offshore oil fields.

7: UK Parliament, North Sea Oil

BRITAIN'S POST-WAR GOVERNMENT nationalized the coal, electricity, gas industries and later nuclear energy plants, all the known sources of power. The British Gas Board learned there were deposits of natural gas under the North Sea. It went drilling for these and discovered deposits of oil which Britain had hitherto imported from overseas. A new source of oil was a new source of wealth, wonderfully exciting to the British, Dutch and Scandinavian nations around its coasts. How could they use it?

Norway, more mountainous than Scotland, has a population of just over 5 million compared to Scotland's 5.25 million. Like Sweden and Denmark its government was elected by folk with egalitarian outlooks, so was a welfare state. The Norwegian government acquired 67% of shares in Statoil, the Norwegian multinational oil and gas company exploiting its offshore wells. It used the revenues to keep and enlarge its social welfare services, and has successfully done so ever since. The United Kingdom's government let its shares be sold on the open market and appointed a British politician to take charge of the process. He at once bought many shares for himself, which was made public by a Scottish newspaper, *The West Highland Free Press*.

The stir this caused made the politician renounce his share. Asked on BBC radio, "But won't your family buy them?" he replied, "My family can do what it wants. If I told them what to do they'd soon tell me to go far enough." (By "far enough" he was politely indicating "to Hell".)

At that time Scotland was losing its main industries, starting with Clydeside shipbuilding. Growing unemployment and a new slogan *IT'S SCOTLAND'S OIL!* resulted in the Scottish National Party getting seven MPs into Westminster in 1974.

At first the companies extracting the oil kept announcing that the oil fields were not very large and would soon run out (an announcement they have kept repeating to this day) and so Ted Heath's Cabinet ordered a secret report on the state of the UK oil fields.

The McCrone Oil Report was delivered and discussed at a secret meeting of Harold Wilson's Cabinet in 1975. It said North Sea oil reserves were larger than estimated and would last decades longer than was alleged by the oil companies, the government and the newspapers. It stated that an independent Scotland "would tend to be in chronic surplus to a quite embarrassing degree and its currency would become the hardest in Europe".

Wilson's Cabinet placed a thirty-year secrecy order on the McCrone Oil Report and continued to put out the story that the oil fields were small and diminishing. When in 2005 (after the required thirty years had elapsed and after a Freedom of

Information Request) the McCrone Oil Report became public, Roy Hattersley, a survivor of that Cabinet, said the Cabinet had suppressed that news because anyone could have discovered the truth for themselves.

In a pre-election manifesto the Labour Party had said it would create an oil fund for the use of Scotland by taxing the companies using wells in Scottish waters. All the other oil-producing states in the world apart from Iraq (for example Texas, Alaska and Arkansas in the USA and Alberta in Canada) maintained an oil fund. Margaret Bain (later Ewing), an SNP member of parliament, asked why Wilson's government had dropped the promise of an oil fund for Scotland mentioned in its pre-election manifesto, and was told from the front bench that her party was "trying to get its snout into the trough". Obviously Labour and Tory politicians only wanted swine like themselves to have snouts in that trough.

Another member of that Labour Cabinet utterly against the idea of an oil fund for the Scots was the Secretary of State for Scotland, Willie Ross, of whom I will say more.

One suggestion discussed during these secret Cabinet meetings was to give the thinly populated Shetland Islands a unique fund from its nearest oil fields so that if Scotland achieved self-government, the Shetlanders would prefer the option of remaining under a Westminster rule. This ongoing oil fund of a penny a barrel has allowed Shetland a generally higher standard of living than in London and anywhere else in our United Kingdom except some millionaire tax-haven Channel Islands.[1]

Since the end of the 19th century a devolved parliament had been occasionally discussed in Westminster. The Labour Party sometimes spoke of it when the Tories were in power, the Conservatives when they were not. Harold Wilson suggested the Scottish Labour Party and trade union chiefs met in London to discuss such a devolved parliament. There was an important football match on the day of the meeting, football is the most widely shared Scottish religion, so too few people turned up. Wilson called another meeting in the Scottish Co-op building, Glasgow, which was well attended. Scots Labour MPs and the Scottish Secretary of State were on the platform; the trade unionists filled the floor. Those on the platform totally rejected the idea of a devolved parliament. By a show of hands the trade unionists were so overwhelmingly for it that there was no point in counting the votes, so the meeting achieved nothing but frustration. Willie Ross had been a schoolteacher and as a politician behaved like the worst kind of teacher, who thinks his class should think and do exactly what he wants. He once told an unsympathetic audience, "*You* don't need a Scottish government! I *am* your Scottish government!" As Secretary of State for Scotland he was responsible for agriculture, fisheries, roads, transport, health and education. The Scots took

---

1. There have been several futuristic novels and one television film showing disastrous states of independent Scotlands. Two show it driven by a Communist plot to make it part of the Soviet Union; another has the Shetlanders also trying for independence and being massacred by the Scots government.

these for granted. Had he been given charge of an oil fund to improve their standard of living they would have argued with him. He enjoyed his unquestioned safety in the House of Commons and later, as Baron Ross of Marnock, joined the even safer Upper House.

When the Scottish National Party almost came to hold the balance of power in Westminster, in 1979 Westminster gave the Scots a referendum on the establishment of their own parliament with certain powers but subordinate to Westminster. Preparations were made for a Yes victory. The former Edinburgh High School on Calton Hill, a masterpiece of 18th-century civic architecture, was chosen as the Scots parliament building-to-be. London BBC sent broadcasters north to manage Scottish broadcasts because a new nation in the UK might be a source of news. In the build-up to the referendum the heads of Tory and Labour Parties appeared in the media explaining that if enough Scots voted for Home Rule, a huge withdrawal of investment from their nation would destroy all its major industries. Despite these threats on a straight Yes or No ballot, the result was 51.6% for the devolved parliament, 48.4% against it, which is how most election results are presented. Of the total electorate, 32.9% voted for a devolved parliament, 30.8% voted against it, the non-voters were 36.4%. But the parliamentary Labour Party had a trick up its sleeve. Months earlier a Scots Labour MP had got the Commons to rule that Scottish devolution would only be granted if 40% of the electors voted for it, so the Home Rule horse won the race by half a head, and therefore lost the race.

A year later a referendum was held in the Canadian province of Quebec to decide, among other things, whether French should be the main language spoken and taught in schools. By a 59.5% majority Quebec voted to keep English its first language. Some of the defeated 40.5% may have believed this outcome was undemocratic because they would have been a majority if non-voters had been counted on their side.

So no parliament was established. But the gloomy future Labour and Tory leaders had prophesied for Scotland in the event of Home Rule still followed the 1979 referendum.

A withdrawal of capital from Scotland destroyed mining, steel, car and textile manufacture here. Apart from those in the whisky industry, Scottish firms transferred their headquarters to their London branches and closed their northern offices and factories. The only people in a position to complain about this were Scottish Labour MPs whose indignation was half-hearted, because they were growing more important to the Labour Party in Westminster as Scotland stopped voting Tory and England became more Conservative. Gradually in Scotland the Tory MPs elected to Westminster dwindled to zero, while in England Margaret Thatcher's eleven-year premiership remained popular and irresistible. In later life Baroness Thatcher was asked about what she thought her greatest achievement and replied, "Tony Blair and New Labour." How smart, how intelligent she was.

For the more right-wing the Tory government grew, the more right-wing became the Labour Party. Its leaders could have reduced the share values of privatized gas, electricity, railways, telephone and water companies by promising to renationalize with minimum compensation when they regained office. They did not. Local Labour councils used Tory laws to sell off public properties. Glasgow's public housing had been almost wholly managed by the Labour Party for over half a century. It had inherited from the Liberals public resources which had almost made it a uniquely independent city-state. It had the earliest municipal pure water supply piped in from Loch Katrine, the first electric lighting of railway stations and streets, the first public telephone system for the use of doctors and hospitals, splendid public parks and (after the Wheatley Acts) more publicly owned housing estates than any local authority outside Greater London. Most of the public parks after Thatcherization remain; hardly anything else. A new manager of Glasgow's housing estates announced that parts had become slums. Instead of working to improve them he left the job and started a consultancy helping folk to buy their own council houses, under a new law making it cheaper to buy these than to buy houses in the private sector. He now had lists of the Glasgow housing stock folk could most profitably buy. In Westminster and in local governments, people drawing salaries as MPs and town councillors could now sell public services and resources to themselves as members of private companies and quangos[2] they were

2. Quango is short for quasi-autonomous non-governmental organization, which means that while being almost (but not quite wholly) responsible for itself, it is supported by taxpayers' money to work for its own and the public good.

creating privately. How could they resist these golden opportunities?

In a 1987 election Alex Salmond, a left-wing Scottish Nationalist, defeated the Conservative candidate for Banff and Buchan, went to Westminster, and first drew attention by an impertinent use of Prime Minister's Question Time. Mrs Thatcher had returned from attending a General Assembly of the Church of Scotland, which she had so annoyed with a speech approving the condition of the poor as underlings, that many ministers walked out before she stopped talking. She had also attended a Glasgow football game where she was welcomed by the manager of Celtic. Salmond asked her if she knew the names of the General Assembly Moderator and the Celtic manager. No experienced politician answers a question exposing their ignorance. She replied that both men were very nice and polite.

For years many Scottish Socialists and even Communists had voted Labour, hoping Labour governments would save what remained of the Welfare State. In 1990 John Major replaced Margaret Thatcher as Prime Minister. After the 1992 general election, a lot of these Socialists and Communists started voting SNP as their only hope of a political change. The election of Tony Blair in 1997 did not alter their minds. I had just published a pamphlet called *Why Scots Should Rule Scotland*, resulting in a phone call from a French newspaper. The editor said the United Kingdom now had a Scottish prime minister with a largely Scottish Cabinet, why should any Scot want a separate parliament for themselves? I told her that any government in Westminster would do only what the banks and London Stock Exchange allowed. In London's Guildhall, Blair's first speech to the chiefs of important British businesses began, "There is a word that must be spoken here. Socialism. Having said it I can now get down to business." Laughter and applause, but not everywhere. Yet Blair's administration decided Scotland would at last have its own parliament to manage everything that had been left to such Secretaries of State as Willie Ross. Donald Dewar, Blair's chosen Secretary of State for Scotland, became Scotland's First Minister. Always an opponent of Scottish Nationalism, he had long before announced that his highest aim in life was to be the Secretary of State for Scotland. Before the 1979 referendum the High School building on Calton Hill had been chosen as the home of the next Scottish parliament. To keep that idea alive, dedicated Nationalists had kept watch in a portacabin beside it, keeping a symbolic flame burning twenty-four hours a day. Donald Dewar announced that a new, modern parliament building would be built for Scotland facing Holyrood Palace, and said, "*That* will be one in the eye for the Scottish Nationalists!"

Dewar was popular and regarded as *A Man of the People* because he appeared and sounded genuinely happy on television and in press interviews. Many were surprised when his death in 2000 showed he had become a millionaire like other Labour leaders. Meanwhile Tony Blair was free to deploy British armed forces to help the Americans to fight wars to keep control of natural resources in Kosovo, Sierra Leone, Iraq and Afghanistan.

The first semi-independent Scottish government was elected under rules of proportional representation not used in Westminster elections. The results were: Labour 56 seats, SNP 35, Conservative 18, Liberal Democrats 17, Greens 1, SSP 1 and Independent (Dennis Canavan) 1. Labour and the Liberal Democrats formed a coalition government.

I had hoped that a Liberal–SNP coalition would re-establish the Welfare State education system John Knox had wanted, post-World War II government had created, Scandinavian nations retained and Thatcher's government abolished. Knox had wanted tax-supported schools in every parish where the children of the richest landlord and labourer would be educated side-by-side, and the cleverest promoted to higher educations. The 1888 compulsory education acts achieved some of this for all children whose parents did not send them to fee-paying schools. Thatcher's government made it legal for parents who could afford special transport for their children to send them to state schools in posher areas than where they lived. The result has been that our state primary and comprehensive schools have become first and second class; and the replacement of state bursaries by bankers' loans for students whose parents cannot afford to pay for their further educations, ensures more financial advantages for them. Thus Scotland would have set the rest of the UK an example of social decency. But at least the Lab–Lib coalition decided not to have England's higher education fees.

And Alex Salmond was gaining authority by his endurance and one fixed idea: a truly independent Scottish parliament. President Clemenceau once said of his political opponents, "They have fewer ideas than I have boots, and ideas are what give men courage." That Salmond leads the party now governing in Scotland is not surprising when we think what political ideas are held by Labour and Tory opponents in Scotland and England. These were summed up by Thiers, an earlier French president who told the electorate, "Enrich yourselves!" President Calvin Coolidge put it another way: "The business of the USA is *business*!" Neither Cameron nor Miliband can use these slogans because they know most of the electorate cannot enrich themselves and have no businesses, so their only policy today is promoting fear of what may follow Scotland achieving an independent parliament. They mock Salmond for refusing to discuss anything that will divide Scotland's electorate. In this he is wise because all important aims will divide Scotland and its politicians as they divide every nation and its elected leaders. Until Scotland has a truly independent government it can achieve nothing except what the City of London with its bankers and brokers allows. Salmond only insists that an independent Scotland have the oil taxation fund which London has given to Shetland and which North America allows to its oil-producing states, and which every oil sheikdom and nation in the Middle East enjoys, apart from Iraq. He also insists that the UK's nuclear submarines and arsenals be taken out of Scotland. The majority of Scots want these things also. When his government makes us a nation again we will argue, quarrel and compromise about important matters. Dividing ourselves over them before that is a waste of time.

I believe that many of the evil things that both Labour and Tory prophesy for Scotland if she gets independence will happen, whether the yes or no campaign wins. As happened after the 1979 referendum, those who predict disasters will try to make them happen, but a Scots parliament with the power of other governments could be a centre of resistance we did not have after 1979, when the independence horse won the race by half a head and therefore lost. But please notice I say an independent Scots parliament *could* be a centre of resistance to City of London economics which have led Westminster to bail out the Royal Bank of Scotland with taxpayers' money and otherwise leave it as it stands instead of nationalizing it. The republic of Iceland jailed four such bank managers for fraud and charged them for the costs of their trial, and in three years the country was recovering from its highly publicized financial crisis. The record of Scotland's ruling SNP government since it took office is discouraging to a patriotic old Scots Socialist. I will say why in chapter ten, 'Scots Anglo-Centralizing'.

8: Settlers and Colonists

SCOTT HAMES IN 2012 asked me to write an essay for a book he was editing: *Unstated: Writers on Scottish Independence*. It was published in the same year, with my essay "Settlers and Colonists". It contained twenty-five other essays by Scottish authors as well known as I am, the book as a whole was barely reviewed, and only my essay received much attention. A journalist from *The Scotsman* phoned me to say his paper was going to use my article. Flattered, I thanked him, thinking it would be extensively quoted or at least summarized. He said, "Of course, you realise it will cause controversy?" I asked, "Why should it?" He said, "A lot of people will resent being called settlers or colonists." I told him I did not see why that should annoy them if they were. He said (perhaps with a touch of jealousy), "There speaks a successful novelist," which ended our conversation. His paper publicized my essay with the headline *ALASDAIR GRAY ATTACKS ENGLISH FOR COLONISING ARTS* and an article paraphrasing a few parts which made me sound like a disgruntled Scottish Colonel Blimp. There was a widespread reaction of the sort called AN OUTCRY which filled inches of newspaper columns for a week or two. I was called a racist and a bigot by folk who had never read my article so did not know they were reacting to a journalist's headline. This led to questions being asked in the Scottish parliament which almost had Nicola Sturgeon, the ruling party's Deputy Leader, apologizing for me. This chapter is an improvement on that essay, starting with a quick summary of matters in the earliest chapters.

On the cover of this book you may have read the slogan 'Outgoers and Incomers Made, Make Every Land'. Both can be divided into settlers or colonists. The Irish tribe that brought Christianity to Pictland and later gave Scotland its name were settlers. So were the Anglo-Saxon invaders who gave England its name, though for a while King Canute regarded England as a province of his Danish empire – a province rather than a colony, because he ruled Danish settlers who were mingling with Anglo-Saxon natives. For centuries Norwegian kings regarded Iceland, Orkney and Shetland as provinces of their empire, but the Western Isles and Sutherland were their colonies because natives, helped by Scots kings, won free of them. A Dutch empire contended on three continents with the British Empire, which ousted the Dutch in Malaysia and North America, where old New York was once New Amsterdam. Only South Africa had enough Dutch settlers to dominate the native majority, survive the Dutch Empire's extinction, and after stout resistance become a British Empire protectorate on their own terms. You probably know what happened later and more recently.

Colonists and settlers may start with the same homeland and some loyalty to it, loyalty dependent on the homeland's support. Differences develop when they have subdued the local natives. In Australia and North America this was done by replacing them, mostly by extermination. In South America the natives were mainly enslaved. Perhaps in New Zealand some of the natives were given equal rights, but for roughly two centuries most subjects of the British Empire were ruled by native Britons employed directly by Westminster. These were colonists who regarded marriage between themselves and local natives as almost unthinkable. Male colonists might take native mistresses, but when Victorian respectability grew fashionable that became rarer and was called *going native*. Hardly any great imperialists united with those they ruled. If successful in one part of the empire they could be sent to work for it in another, before finally retiring to their homeland, which they sometimes helped to govern. The Duke of Wellington, an Irish general in the Indian army, was sent to fight Napoleon's empire in Europe and later had a spell as Britain's prime minister.

The USA has made such imperialism a thing of the past. It does not exploit foreign lands by planting settlers, like Britain in Canada and Australia, or sending governors with British armed forces as in India and Kenya. The USA has obtained governments that trade with it on its own terms by bribing dictatorships in South America, the Middle East and Africa. When elected governments intended to use their own natural resources, the CIA replaced them with dictatorships in Guatemala, Chile and Iran, where the coup was managed with secret

British support. From the Arctic Circle to Turkey the USA surrounded the USSR with air force bases which remain to this day. They are manned by a new kind of colonist: American servicemen like those who once manned the Polaris submarine base on the Firth of Clyde, and now man another with more destructive potential on Loch Long. Though set up to defend the rest of the world from attack by the Soviet Union, they are now supposed to defend it from international terrorists, but did not prevent the destruction of the New York Trade Center eleven years after the USSR disbanded. In the 1990s the USA withdrew their air force base from Greenham Common in England, partly because of strong local protests by the English, most of them women. The United States NATO bases in Coulport and on the Isle of Lewis have aroused no local protests the British press and broadcasters think worth reporting. They may slightly boost the local economy in thinly peopled places.

Ambitious folk are inclined to seek a better life in richer nations, even when not driven from their homelands by famine, as were 19th-century Irish, or by landlords who could make more money out of sheep, as were Scots Highlanders. But others have prospered by voluntary emigration, and Scots have usually gone to England and her former overseas colonies, for until recently their higher standard of public education made better jobs there possible. For two and a half centuries colonists and settlers from Scotland and Ireland helped the London government create and rule a vast empire, while Scots Lowlanders cultivated their fertile districts and used local deposits of iron and coal to develop their own industries. Until the 1960s we exported manufactures as well as people. Those in the Highlands and Western Isles were unluckier, being driven overseas by landlords helped by the police and sometimes the Royal Navy. When North Britain became reachable by railway and steam ship many southerners came here, and have been coming ever since.

But after 1918 they came to a Scotland managed by folk who increasingly thought their homeland a province, which the 18th- and 19th-century Scots industrialists, scholars, scientists and authors did not. After 1918 the Scottish iron and shale oil deposits were exhausted, and a generation of brave and intelligent minds had been killed or depressed by World War I. After the Treaty of Versailles came more and more unemployment in a Scotland which many fine intelligences abandoned by getting work in London or overseas. Their homeland was left to folk with less and less confidence in fellow Scots with original ideas English elites might not appreciate. This did not discourage immigration *into* Scotland. By the 1970s the long list of Scots doing well in the south was over-balanced by English with high positions in Scottish electricity, water supply, property development, universities, local civil services and art galleries. As in other places, English settlers in Scotland are as true a part of it as the Irish who escaped here from famine, and dug canals, railway lines and reservoirs; the Italians escaping from the phylloxera that destroyed their vineyards and who brought us ice-cream and fish-and-chip parlours; the Jews escaping pogroms in

Russia and elsewhere who entered many professions; the Indians and Chinese from former imperial colonies who became restaurateurs and shopkeepers. These are now part of Scottish culture. English settlers have also done us good. Through being an author I know of scholars and artists among these. People in healthcare, scientific research and education will know of others, but I'll start with only four of those I know.

Edward Dwelly (1864–1939) was an Englishman who became a bagpiper in the army, an Ordinance Survey employee, and made himself such a Gaelic scholar that, seeing that no good dictionary of the Gaelic language existed, like Doctor Johnson making one for the English language in the 1750s, he created one that is still, with small later additions, the best in use. His work upon it was not funded by publishers as Johnson's was, nor could he afford to employ assistants. He learned the trade of printing and typeset it all by hand. Like others who became printers without being first apprenticed to the trade (inventors of good typefaces, Cardinal Bembo, William Morris, Eric Gill) he was an innovator, who invented a swivelling seat that abolished standing while setting a page. Printers adopted that until typesetting by computer keyboard abolished them too. He was not enriched by this great work for a language which English readers and scholars thought was dying. Only Gaels and a few folk like Dwelly knew the greatness of its poetry, but he was the one scholar who ensured their language did not die.

Frank Newbery (1855–1946), born in Devon, was a painter when being an artist was a qualification for arts administration. He directed Glasgow School of Art from 1885 to 1918 and transformed it from what has been called a "traditionally organized municipal art school into an internationally recognized centre for modern art education. During his regime Glasgow was to develop as one of the most dynamic centres for the production of art and design in Europe, eclipsing Edinburgh's long-standing reputation as the artistic capital of Scotland." He rejected the idea that drawing and painting had nothing to learn from, nothing to give to the crafts of pottery, textile, furniture design and architecture. He employed Charles Rennie Mackintosh to design his masterpiece, the Glasgow School of Art building, greatly to the annoyance of other Glasgow architects (good ones in traditional styles) who resented the work of Mackintosh being acclaimed in Italian and German art centres. Mackintosh's unique designs included furniture, lettering and (modern novelties in the 1900s) electric clocks and light-fittings. When Timothy Neat showed this building to John Berger recently, Berger said of Mackintosh, "He could have designed a whole civilization." Yet in the 1950s when I was an art student in Glasgow and architecture was a big part of the first two years of the General Arts Course our lecturers never mentioned the architect of the building we occupied! For decades Mackintosh was widely ignored in both Scotland and England as an Art Nouveau eccentric like Aubrey Beardsley and whoever designed the Paris Metro entrances, until Nikolaus Pevsner rediscovered him, not before some of his achievements in Glasgow had been vandalized or looted.

John McGrath (1935–2002) was born near Liverpool to an Irish family and first became a playwright who wrote the earliest scripts of *Z Cars*. He wanted to create a popular form of radical theatre like Joan Littlewood's Theatre Workshop, which among other things had produced *Oh What a Lovely War*. He wrote *The Cheviot, the Stag and the Black, Black Oil*, an often funny, politically accurate play about the Scottish Highlands from the 19th-century Clearances to the extraction of North Sea oil. This dealt with how landlords (usually Scottish) and politicians (mostly English) exploited the native Highlanders and Islanders, so he came to Scotland and helped to found the 7:84 Theatre Company, a title to remind us that in 1973 7% of the UK's people owned 84% of its wealth. (In 2014 the smaller percentage has engrossed more from the rest.) This hugely successful play was taken on a tour through the Highlands and Lowlands. The 7:84 group kept performing his plays until 2008, when it ceased with some other small theatre companies and local magazines when the Scottish Arts Council withdrew financial support, but the company left several experienced actors and one director who still flourish.

Timothy Neat from Cornwall is another English settler who has also publicized and aided the work of Scots too left-wing and intellectual to be popular here: the poet and political activist Hugh MacDiarmid and the poet, songwriter, folklore preserver and political activist Hamish Henderson. From his base as lecturer in Duncan of Jordanstone College of Art and

Design, Dundee, he has made four award-winning films: *Hallaig* about Gaelic poet Sorley MacLean, *The Liberty Tree* about Hamish Henderson, *The Summer Walkers* about Scotland's travelling folk, and *Play Me Something*, set on the island of Barra, with John Berger, Tilda Swinton, Hamish Henderson and Liz Lochhead. His friendship with Berger is only one proof that his Scottish interests have not made him parochial. As Tom Leonard has written: "THE LOCAL IS THE INTERNATIONAL. THE NATIONAL IS THE PAROCHIAL."

These four remarkable immigrants, including the anarchist Guy Aldred mentioned earlier, supported Scottish culture and its best representatives when the comfortable middle-class Scottish majority preferred to forget, ignore or disparage them. France, Germany and most independent nations have accepted that what Ibsen called "the damned Liberal majority", sometimes called the *bourgeoisie*, will dislike seriously imaginative and creative people, so only a minority will encourage them unless they become fashionable. In dictatorships they are taken so seriously that those not murdered have had to escape abroad. But in Scotland folk in the highest places were all in England, and the high heid yins left in Scotland were so parochial that many of our most creative found their best supporters were English outsiders. More good settlers in Scotland will be mentioned, but here are a few I regard as colonists, and it is important to remember that these incomers were appointed to high positions in Scottish cultural institutions by highly respected Scottish committees.

Giles Havergal was born in 1938, Edinburgh, *"educated at Harrow and Oxford, became assistant stage manager of Carlisle Repertory Theatre, joined the Old Vic as an actor. In 1969 he became director of Glasgow's Citizens Theatre. With Robert David MacDonald and Philip Prowse he transformed a local repertory theatre into one of the UK's foremost theatres, producing a strong mix of English and European classical and modern work."* That almost straight quotation from *Chambers Scottish Biographical Dictionary* has only three words with which I disagree. The Citizens Theatre was not a simple "local repertory theatre" before Giles took it over.

Ever since 1904 when Yeats and Lady Gregory founded the Abbey Theatre in Dublin, Scots with a love of plays had been trying to follow their example by starting a Scottish national theatre. The Irish founders were not interested in Oscar Wilde and Bernard Shaw whose plays were doing well in London's West End. They began a tradition of playwriting that flourished so that Ireland in world literature (as an American told Roddy Doyle) "punches well above its weight". After World War II the Glasgow playwright James Bridie thought he had achieved a Scottish national theatre by persuading Glasgow City Council to subsidize the Citizens, which began by successfully producing Scottish plays by himself (who had then written London West End successes), also by David MacLennan, Joe Corrie and other Scots. These were performed along with plays by Shakespeare, Ibsen, Brecht, Frisch and Irishmen Synge to Friel. His Citizens gave a start to fine actors such as Duncan Macrae and Helen Mirren. After Giles Havergal became a director for thirty-four years his excellent productions used only two plays by Scots, one being *Trainspotting* adapted by his friend Harry Gibson from a popular novel. He was supported in this policy by Jan McDonald, a member of the Citizens board and lecturer in drama at Glasgow University, who was outspoken in her belief that Scotland would never produce a good playwright. Nor did he promote Scottish acting, because out of season he planned and auditioned for his productions in his London home. I call him a colonist reluctantly, as we always talked politely to each other, and he once employed me to design and paint scenery for a stage version of *A Clockwork Orange*.

When the Scottish Arts Council started after World War II its chief members were the playwright James Bridie and novelist Naomi Mitchison. They met alternately in Glasgow or Edinburgh hotel rooms, with a minutes secretary as almost their only bureaucracy. There is no room to describe how that Council became bigger and operated wholly from Edinburgh, but in 1974 it funded the Third Eye Arts Centre in Glasgow with Tom McGrath (no relative of the 7:84 founder) to direct it, though he too was a playwright, musician, and one of the team behind the success of *The Great Northern Welly Boot Show*. Under his guidance it became (said the *Guardian*) "a shrine of the avant-garde". After five years of promoting the work of artists from at home and abroad Tom retired to concentrate on his own arts.

The Scottish Arts Council appointed Chris Carrell who, after a brave beginning, made his job easier by putting other English in charge of the centre's shows, folk without knowledge or much respect for any artists not celebrated in London or abroad. When the Third Eye Centre went bankrupt in 1992 no Scottish artists spoke up for it. But when Chris went south to another job in England he had given work experience to several English arts administrators who had gone back to jobs in their homeland.

Most of Scotland is understandably sick of the Strathclyde region, which certainly contains roughly a quarter of the Scottish people, talking as if it were the whole of it, which I, a Glaswegian, cannot help doing. My one excuse is that much I complain of in Glasgow – its provincialization by a local government without knowledge or interest in its history and culture – can be found elsewhere in places between the Orkneys and Carlisle, so I will continue raving about my home town for some more pages.

From 1880 to 1937 Glasgow staged four big international exhibitions of manufactures and arts in which Scottish culture and Glasgow itself were strongly represented. How could they not be? It had been the second-biggest industrial city in the British Empire. In 1937 it may have been overtaken by Manchester, but it was still Britain's biggest exporter of steam ships, railway trains and much else, and was slowly recovering from the terrible unemployment of the 1930s because the long-postponed threat of war with Germany was at last being accepted as likely, although unwelcome, so steel production and coal mines in Lanarkshire were again essential to Clydeside ship building and locomotive works, which again renewed life throughout World War II.

In those years Scotland had not come to feel parochial. In 1990 Thatcher's government chose Glasgow to be the United Kingdom's first European Capital of Culture, partly because Glasgow Labour Council promised that if it got the job it would not ask for a government subsidy. Glasgow's council rented the best English arts administrators money could rent, and gave them control of Glasgow's main concert halls, theatres and galleries. They did not organize a drama festival of successful plays by Strathclyde authors: Bridie's *Mr Bolfry*, McLellan's *Jamie the Saxt*, Ena Lamont Stewart's *Men Should Weep* or Archie Hind's Scottish version of the *The Ragged Trousered Philanthropists*. The last could have been staged by its original director, David Hayman. They could have commissioned an original stage play from John Byrne or Peter McDougall, successful stage and television authors who might have co-operated with Billy Connolly to create something new, like *The Great Northern Welly Boot Show*. They could have had a festival of documentary films by Grierson, animated films by Norman McLaren made for the Canadian Film Board, short films by Eddie McConnell, even a history of 20th-century Glasgow put together from the Scottish Film Archive. They could have arranged shows of painting in Kelvingrove Museum and elsewhere from those late 20th-century artists called

the Glasgow Boys through the school of Colourists around J.D. Fergusson while taking in the best work of those 20th-century individualists John Quinton
Pringle, James Cowie, Robert Colquhoun, Robert MacBryde and Joan Eardley. But Glasgow's Labour Council had appointed the English Julian Spalding, chosen by Janey Buchan as head of Glasgow art galleries, and other administrators who were equally ignorant of anything good that had been made here. To them, as to most of our Labour councillors, Glasgow's past was a tale of working-class Socialism and gang violence which should be forgotten. New Labour wanted their City of Culture to attract foreign tourists and investors, so performances and shows were brought in from outside Scotland, and hardly anything Glaswegian was presented when Glasgow was the European Capital of Culture.

By explaining these things my essay "Settlers and Colonists" got some to call me a racist bigot, which did not hurt because I did not believe them. In my one letter to the press on the matter I explained that I thought Nick Barley (director of the Edinburgh International Book Festival) and Vicky Featherstone (then director of the Scottish National Theatre) and Simon Groom (director of the Scottish National Gallery of Modern Art) and Ben Harman (then director of the Glasgow Gallery of Modern Art) were good settlers of whom I approved because, although English, they had funded a play or exhibited pictures of mine. I had been thinking of the first director of Creative Scotland, an organisation by which the Scottish government had replaced the old Scottish Arts Council, and the first curator of the recently built Robert Burns Birthplace Museum in Dumfries. On getting their jobs the first had announced he knew little about Scottish culture but was looking forward to learning about it; the second had said he did not know much about Robert Burns but looked forward to learning. At the 2013 Edinburgh Book Festival I had a friendly public discussion about these matters with Nick Barley, which seemed to amuse the audience. It brought me the following letter which I quote in full, with my reply, in a chapter of its own.

9: A Small Stir
of Correspondence

the National Trust
for Scotland
a place for everyone

Mr A Gray

19th August 2013

Dear Mr Gray,

I refer to recent comments attributed to you on BBC News online where it was reported that in the course of your Edinburgh Book Festival appearance on 15 August you made "scathing" remarks about Nat Edwards and RBBM. If this is true (and I hope it is not) I am concerned that you might question the credentials of the Director of the Robert Burns Birthplace Museum by virtue of his country of origin.

Being brought up in Scotland to respect and promote the values of a tolerant & free society, I am embarrassed by the message being sent. Freedom of speech is also valued but rarely respected if simply a cover for rudeness. In marked contrast, I am proud to observe the apologies that fellow Scots have been compelled to offer to our Director, Nat Edwards and the enthusiasm expressed to disassociate from the remarks.

Your underlying message is understood. However your own reported test of a settler's entitlement to represent and promote Scottish culture is "how much they identify with the culture of the place and work to promote it on the basis of understanding it". By that measure Nat Edwards passes your test with distinction as amply demonstrated through award panels, satisfied visitors, academics & commentators.

I trust you enjoyed the Trust's hospitality when you were invited to the launch of the new RBBM and are appreciative of our promotion & sale of your works through our retail outlets. In keeping with our proud national traditions of tolerance & hospitality I have resisted calls to withdraw your merchandise from our shelves and simply ask for your respect and courtesy in return.

Yours sincerely,

Pete Selman
Director of Properties & Visitor Services

My reply is as follows.

Thursday, 22 August 2013

Dear Pete Selman,

Thank you for your letter of the 19th. At the Edinburgh Book Festival I did indeed say that the curator of the Burns Museum remarked on accepting the post that he did not know much about Robert Burns but looked forward to learning of him. In this I was quoting a news item, and confess not to recall which paper printed it. If you tell me the report was false and Nat Edwards was chosen because he had more than a casual knowledge of Burns, then I owe him an apology. Please email me if I am wrong in thinking he said such a thing and I certainly will make a public apology to him.

If the report was accurate, it still annoys me that the job did not go to an applicant with more knowledge of Burns, whether American, Russian or Japanese. But perhaps the only folk who applied were English and Scots, in which case I announce a personal prejudice.

One rejected applicant was Elspeth King, who, when curator of the People's Palace Local History Museum in 1977, made me Glasgow's official Artist Recorder. From the People's Palace being one of Scotland's least visited museums she made it one of the most. The Carnegie Foundation later employed her to create a completely new local history museum for Dunfermline. After that she became curator of the Smith Art Gallery and Museum in Stirling and has made that equally successful. Like most Scots of working-class origin (her dad was a Fife coalminer) she is a Burns enthusiast. As curator of the Burns Museum she would certainly have displayed evidence of Burns' support of parliamentary reform at home and the French Revolution abroad, which I did not see when there at the opening. While in the People's Palace during the 1980s miners' national strike she put on an exhibition about the earlier national strike of the 1920s. Perhaps this suggested she had the same left-wing opinions that originally created the Labour Party. In Stirling she was also responsible for printing *The Wallace Muse*, a book of poems inspired by the life and legend of William Wallace. Though partly funded by the Scottish Arts Council this could be taken as a support for Scottish Independence, which is why Scotland's National Museum contains hardly any memorials of Wallace, and is probably why representatives of the Labour Party, Lottery Fund, Scottish Government and National Trust preferred a decent man without much knowledge of Burns and no wish to indicate his radical politics. If I am right, then I believe the appointment was made by the same anti-Scottish prejudice that appointed as head of Creative Scotland an Englishman who said he knew very little about Scottish culture but looked forward to learning it.

You may regard this letter as another piece of intolerant rudeness, and even Anglophobia. No. I object as little to English immigrants working in Scotland as I do to Scots emigrants working abroad. The majority are among the poorest workers, a class nowadays including schoolteachers and National

Health employees. Their influence on the lands where they work is small enough to be unimportant. I cannot put heads of Scottish cultural establishments into that category, not because they are better paid, but because I think folk with a leading part in Scottish cultural institutions should have more than casual knowledge of Scottish culture.

I am friendly with Nick Barley (Director of the Edinburgh Book Festival), Simon Groom (Curator of the Scottish Gallery of Modern Art), Ben Harman (Curator of the Glasgow Gallery of Modern Art) and Vicky Featherstone (former Director of Scotland's National Theatre). All are English, but all have promoted my work, so I put them into the category of Good Settlers who know enough about Scottish literature and art to belong here. But is it not strange that hardly any significant local or Scottish organizations have Scots in charge? My words have brought letters to the press from some who argue that Scotland has no worthwhile culture so can achieve nothing without English administrators. In literature and other art forms this is obviously untrue. Is it Anglophobic to suggest that, as the Irish administer their own cultural affairs within the Republic and the folk of Ulster administer theirs within the nine counties, some Scots may be equally capable within the frontiers of their homeland?

I admit I am in some matters a Scotophobe, which may be because my mother's parents were English. The committees who choose English administrators in their homeland mostly contain bankers, brokers and politicians who regard the City of Westminster as their

Capital in every sense of the word, so mainly oppose any assertion of Scottish independence. That many English here will certainly vote for independence won't stop Scottish brokers thinking that the English *they* employ will not. It is not surprising that the head of Edinburgh International Festival is banning all productions dealing with Scottish politics in the 2014 EIF shortly before the referendum.

I did indeed enjoy the Trust's hospitality when you invited me to speak at the launch of the new Robert Burns Birthplace Museum. The sandwiches and wine were very nice. I am grateful for you resisting calls to withdraw my merchandise from your shelves. Can you tell me exactly which of my merchandise is currently on them? Since 1981 I have had over twenty books of novels, stories, poems and plays published, but never imagined some were for sale among the souvenirs in National Trust properties. Please tell me which these are. My wife sells some of these books and complains that she has had no orders from the Scottish National Trust, but she is not the only supplier of my work. I enclose a stamped, addressed envelope for the convenience of your reply.

Yours truly,

Alasdair Gray

POSTSCRIPT On visiting an exhibition in Pollock House, Glasgow, I was given a lift homeward by a very friendly employee of the Scottish National Trust, who told me he had the recent pleasure of refusing a job application by Sean Connery. The actor had heard your Trust would soon have a museum on Bannockburn with

a recorded voice lecturing on it, and had offered to give his voice free. He did not need to say that he had
rejected the actor because, like Bruce and Salmond, Connery wanted Scottish Independence. I do not know how the Bannockburn Museum will avoid the subject, but where there is a will there is a way. I am sure the Trust will not be so tactless as to pay an English actor for his voice, but I may be wrong.

Mr Selman did not reply to this letter, which indicates that Mr Edwards did announce his determination to learn more about Burns now that he was curator of the Robert Burns Birthplace Museum and had nothing to do with setting up its displays. I saw them before consuming sandwiches, biscuits and wine which the museum hospitably offered its speakers before the opening. I said nothing that could have offended the audience on that occasion, but mentioned Burns' radical politics and his support of the French Revolution and parliamentary reform. No displays in the museum showed the political context of his times and his attitude to it, which had his popular poems *A Man's a Man for A' That* and *Robert Bruce's Address to his Troops at Bannockburn,* otherwise known as *Scots Wha Hae*, damned as rabble-rousing by Tory critics in the early 19th century. I will be pleasantly surprised to learn that the RBBM now has a display correcting that omission.

10: Scots
Anglo-Centralizing

NOT NOSTALGIA FORCES THOSE who think hard about Scotland these days to keep recalling the 1707 Treaty of Union, because four terms of that treaty decided how folk in Scotland would live, and violation of them by Westminster has decided and is still deciding much more. The terms were: Scotland should keep its traditional laws; no Scots soldiers should be sent abroad against their will by the British government; that the Scots Presbyterian Kirk should keep its constitution; that the Scottish legal system would not be changed by the London parliament.

VIOLATION 1: The Scots in Westminster soon found that in all except criminal law, anything that was of disadvantage to English trade was overruled. English brokers were free to treat Ireland as an English colony, and got a government subsidy to develop the Irish linen industry. They began buying Scottish flax for it. Scots MPs protested that this broke one of the Treaty of Union terms, because Scots law forbad the export of Scottish flax because this would impoverish Scottish weavers. On this and similar matters, here are the replies they got from the London parliament.

"Whatever are or may be the laws of Scotland, now she is subject to the sovereignty of England, she must be governed by English laws."

"Have we not bought the Scots and the right to tax them?"

"We have catcht Scotland and will keep her fast."

Changes of law in England were given force in Scotland by an enabling clause which said, in effect, *This goes for Scotland too.* But in criminal matters the Scots legal system mainly stayed intact until the 20th and 21st century which will be discussed in the fourth violation.

VIOLATION 2: The Black Watch regiment had been recruited in the Lowlands to keep the Highland clans in order. In the mid-1740s it marched to London, being told that the king wanted to review his loyal Scottish regiment. In London they were told that the king was not in London just now, but the regiment would be shipped to the West Indies, where the death rate for Europeans through fever was very high. (This was a good argument for using African slaves there.) The Black Watch mutinied. A hundred were marching back to Scotland when they were arrested by an English army under General Wade, court martialed and sentenced to death, but only two corporals and a private were executed. The rest, suitably cowed, were marched back to London then shipped abroad to Gibraltar, Georgia and the West Indies.

The last person to give the Treaty of Union as a reason to reject military orders was Michael Grieve, Hugh MacDiarmid's son, in 1953. He rejected conscription for the statutory two years of National Service in those days, because conscripts were sent to Cyprus and parts of Africa where natives were still subject to British rule. Scottish judges decided that that clause of the Union

Treaty had long been out of date, and sent Grieve to Barlinnie jail.

VIOLATION 3: The Scottish Kirk's constitution had been democratic, in that the minister of each parish was chosen by a committee of elders in the congregation from two or three ordained by other ministers in their district, or presbytery as it was called. In England, just as the monarch or prime minister chose the archbishop and bishops, the chief landowner chose the local vicar or parish priest from anyone who had passed through Oxford or Cambridge, giving the job to a friend or relation. Scottish landowners started doing the same, to the great annoyance of many in their parishes, but the practice continued, causing small breakaway congregations until the great Disruption of 1843. Much might be said of that. Too few care for the Scots Kirk nowadays and I say no more.

VIOLATION 4: The English legal system is mainly based upon precedent, Scots law, like French law, was based on principle taken over from the Roman legal code derived from Justinian. Most codes of law do good if administered by fair-minded people, but all incline to favour the wealthy because *The Poor Had No Lawyers*. They could not afford them before the late 1940s when the British government allowed them Legal Aid, which is now being phased out. The five italicized words are the title of Andy Wightman's book, subtitled *Who Owns Scotland (And How They Got It)*, an argument for a Scots government helping crofters and cultivators of small farms get ownership of the land they work. Every member of the Scottish parliament should read this book. (So should English MPs.)

The biggest change to Scots law followed the defeat of the 1745 Jacobite invasion of England by a mainly Highland force, which hoped to succeed with English support, but finding they retreated back to Scotland without a battle, having done nothing worse than cause a brief panic on the London Stock Exchange. The British parliament passed laws to break the power of the Gaelic clans, though some of these had fought against the Jacobites. This power had traditionally depended on the loyalties of clansmen to their chief, and readiness to fight for him. In the Highlands and parts of the Lowlands some leaders of great families had inherited the right to overrule some laws at their own discretion. These rights were abolished, though many Scots lords in Westminster and lawyers in Edinburgh fought to keep them. The wearing of the kilt and tartan was banned, though a loophole in the law allowed them to be worn by tenants of chiefs who recruited them into regiments fighting for the Empire abroad. The full effect of these measures was seen in the 19th century, when chiefs had become mere landlords who regarded their people as tenants and cottars. Whole townships of crofters were now evicted from glens and islands where more money could be made by sheep farming or renting out for shooting.

In the 20th century the Westminster government sometimes used the Scottish legal difference to test an Act in the north before applying it to England. When World War I began, pubs could open and close as early and late as the landlords wanted. Westminster decided that folk in munitions factories were losing hours of work by drinking too much, and introduced strict opening and closing hours which lasted until the 1980s. Margaret Thatcher's government first allowed Scottish landlords to choose their own opening and closing times, and we were so pleased that a year later she did the same in England. When she imposed her poll tax on Scotland there were many demonstrations against it here, but they were peaceful and did not annoy many folk. When brought to England a year later it caused riots, shop windows were smashed and private property looted, so the tax was withdrawn. With its devolved parliament Scotland is no longer a testing ground for advancing Westminster legislation, but the erosion of Scots law has been continuous and commented on by Andrew Dewar Gibb in *Law from over the Border*.

Astonishingly Alex Salmond's Cabinet Secretary for Justice, Kenny MacAskill, has used the Scots parliament's "devolved" powers, not to keep our different legal system but to bring Scottish criminal procedure into almost complete agreement with that of England. This has been done in two ways.

Once, each country had safeguards the other lacked. In England these derived from legal precedent. Scots prohibitions to prevent miscarriages of justice included corroboration in criminal cases, the best evidence rule, the value of circumstantial evidence and the Not Proven verdict. Nearly all senior judges in Scotland opposed the abolition of corroboration.

They are now compelled to accept it. The independent public prosecution service has been swallowed by the organization called the Crown Office & Procurator Fiscal Service. This makes it similar to the Crown Prosecution Service in England where the police instigate the prosecutions, but in England someone can withdraw a complaint. In Scots law this has never been allowed, and the Fiscal Service office, which once prided itself on its independence of the police force, is now partly staffed by many serving or retired police officers, and, lacking independent prosecutors, is biased toward the prosecution and against the defenders.

Our devolved Justice Department is also cutting down our former legal system. The Scottish Bar is being destroyed by decisions to prosecute cases once dealt with in the High Court at the level of sheriff and jury, while sheriffs' powers are increased to giving sentences of up to five years. There is also an unusual downgrading of criminal offences. Cases once prosecuted in the Sheriff Court are sometimes given a fixed penalty, or "red penned" *No Pro*, meaning do not prosecute. If someone assaults you in Sauchiehall Street and the police decide your injury is not very serious, there may be no further legal proceedings. That is why the Scots justice system boasts that there has been a significant drop in criminal activity, because the Scottish High Court has thus reduced its number of cases by 30%. So many crimes are no longer prosecuted that Scots newspapers report that the police war on crime is being won. Untrue.

That the trend is to remove access to justice from many victims and the accused is shown by the closure of local law courts and local police stations, following the recent merger of all local police forces into one, against the outspoken advice of several police chiefs. The consequences were made public at the start of April 2014 by Graeme Pearson, a member of the Scottish parliament and of the Labour Justice Committee. He is also a former police officer who says:

"Police staff have been axed in their thousands, police officer numbers began to drop, police stations and control rooms across Scotland have closed. More and more officers are sitting behind desks doing paperwork; they should be out on the streets catching criminals.

Now we find out that police officers, under pressure from their bosses, are fiddling figures. Local communities are losing their voice about how they are policed. That isn't what we voted for in parliament.

With a new police computer system running dangerously over budget, a threat of strike action by police staff and millions being paid out for ill-health early retirements, Police Scotland isn't a happy place to be. Things need to change and Scottish Labour is committed to ensuring that our national police force is locally accountable and responsive. Unless that happens, the problems facing Police Scotland won't be tackled and can only get worse."

Add to this the fact that if you enter a police station with a complaint, a poster tells you to make it by way of the World Wide Web. This means those without a digital keyboard or ability to use one – elderly, blind and poor people – cannot now complain effectively.

That is another reason why Scots prosecutions for crime have diminished.

While crimes against people who can be dismissed as unimportant are being ignored, other potential crimes have been enlarged by new laws. Many have clauses which can only be called Kafkaesque, so liable are they to bizarre interpretations. For instance, the Criminal Justice and Licensing (Scotland) Act 2010 lets anyone with a grievance against someone report them to the police, who may arrest the person accused and put them on trial without them, or their defence lawyer, knowing who has accused them. Where there is suspicion of terrorism those conducting the trial can carry out legal procedures unknown to the accused and their defenders. For example, the prosecutor may appoint a lawyer to hear part of the case and someone to represent the defence without telling the accused that this is happening. There is a provision in the Act for an appeal, but how can you appeal against a procedure if you don't know it has taken place? This state was described by Kafka in his novel *The Trial*, and Scottish law now allows it. Alex Salmond's government enacted it with hardly one of the SNP questioning or opposing.

The Act also creates a new offence by redefining the old common law conspiracy offence. Anyone in contact with someone charged with a serious organized crime can be arrested, because "there needs to be no corroboration in respect of such a serious charge. Evidence from one person saying another person is involved is enough." This abolishes corroboration in one of the most serious new crimes in the Scottish statute book, yet the Act making this law is worded so vaguely that almost anyone who knows someone charged with a crime can be arrested as an accomplice without corroboration and undergo a penalty of fourteen years. More sinister is criminalizing the failure of anyone to report what they think *may become* a "serious organized crime". No matter how flimsy you think your reasons for suspecting someone of being connected to a "serious organized crime", not telling a policeman could get you five years in jail. Of course the lawyer employed by the accused is exempted, but the Act replaces the common law crime of conspiracy with this crazy crime instead. It means that if a secretary working for the defence lawyer types out a statement while preparing a defence for the accused, and does not give a copy to the police, she or he can be held guilty and jailed for five years. Many solicitors agree that this will lead to miscarriages of justice.

There is also a peculiarly Scottish section of this Act, applying to objects taken in and out of jail. Previous laws guarded against the movement of drugs and offensive weapons. The new Act adds to these tape recorders and mobile phones which lawyers use to defend their clients.

Scotland had a breach of the peace law widely accepted as efficient, but section 38 of the new Act widens its scope. Anyone accused of behaving in a "threatening or abusive" manner causing fear and alarm can be jailed for five years if a court finds them guilty. Recently a woman who told off a child who had attacked *her* child was tried for that crime. The sheriff threw the case out of court, but he must have known that newspaper publicity would have been on his side in that case. Section 38 is now (April 2014) at the Appeal Court for clarification. Nowadays newspapers widely assume that anyone charged with a crime, especially sexual abuse, must be guilty of it. Some mentally disturbed folk charged with such a crime have been beaten up by fellow prisoners before a fair trial has found them guilty of it. Many fiscals, sheriffs and justices of peace spring to the same conclusions as the newspapers. They are human, like the rest of us, but do not feel as human as the accused. This also seriously applies in matters of mental illness.

The Thatcher government started the reduction of money to state-supported psychiatric hospitals, resulting in the closure of some and the premature discharge of many patients from others. This policy has continued and increased under later governments, including Scotland's. The impact is hardest on the mental health services, because the greatest part of the public would rather not think about those who were once called mad, despite the fact that some years ago an Audit Scotland report suggested that one in four Scots are diagnosed with a mental illness at some point in their lives. Sufferers are now chiefly described as having Borderline Personality Disorder, which sounds less serious. Those called upon to judge an arrested person's sanity in court are community psychiatric nurses, CPNs for short. That Glasgow Sheriff Court has CPNs on duty on

Monday, Wednesday and Friday from 9 a.m. till noon shows how little our courts regard mental illness. The upshot is that a seriously disturbed person charged with a crime *may* receive counselling from a CPN and occasional visits to a psychiatrist, but is seldom treated as if their mental state influenced their crime. If they can stand up in a witness box, know who the prime minister is, and can tell the difference between pleading guilty and not guilty, they are usually judged sane, found guilty and penalized, regardless of how weird their behaviour has been and how dangerous their delusions. The result? When the Douglas Inch Psychiatric Unit examined prisoners in Glasgow's Barlinnie jail, it decided one third were mentally ill and 10% so ill that they should be hospitalized. That finding was never acted upon, that research never repeated. In 2012 the Barlinnie jail governor, Derek McGill, wrote a *Herald* article saying that 260 of his 1,100 prisoners had mental health problems, but he never had any transferred to hospitals.

Among recent cases of those diagnosed sane and fit to plead was a man who thought himself a garden gnome. He gained entry to a hospital for contagious diseases, and he explained that he meant to use the blood of the patients to poison those in churches whose tenets he disagreed with. He was not diagnosed as suffering a severe mental illness until he attempted to murder his mother and wrap her in a carpet.

More recently, a man who believed vampires hovered outside his second-floor flat, who fried and ate the blood and brains of pigeons, and who said he wished to skin his dog to see what it was like inside, and who claimed to have killed and eaten a flatmate, was diagnosed as having Borderline Personality Disorder, and therefore deemed sane and fit to plead.

Ben is ex-army, and has been diagnosed as suffering from Post-traumatic Stress Disorder. He believes the concierge of his council flat has bored holes into his room, to monitor his behaviour. He has repeatedly sought help from several agencies, but it is hard to converse with him as he rushes words together to the extent of incoherence. One of these agencies was the police, who first warned him to stop pestering them, and have now charged him with two breaches of the law because he went on complaining to them.

Of course all this legal maltreatment of the mentally ill is justified on financial grounds, but what is the economic value of not treating people who can be a danger to the public? The danger is occurring more and more. In early March 2014 a man discharged from hospital was clearly so ill that he attacked and killed a complete stranger on a bus. A society where psychiatric hospitals are being driven to discharge such folk for financial reasons has seriously degenerated, especially when its police stations and law courts are being reduced, new laws allow what were recently grievous crimes to be ignored, and allow almost anyone to be arrested without proof because someone suspects them of a serious crime, without them ever knowing their accuser. Former police states like Germany and Russia found it convenient to assume everyone was guilty unless they could prove their innocence. This looks like happening here in a Scotland where the police have recently suggested local governments be abolished! What was once thought a branch of local government now wishes to replace it! If that succeeds, Scotland will certainly be a police state.

All independent thinkers should look hard at what is happening here. In an earlier chapter I said that an independent Scots parliament would contain many groups disagreeing, attacking and compromising with each other over important issues. What if I am wrong? What if Scotland's elected members of parliament want to do nothing but draw fat salaries, think as little as possible about managing North Britain fairly, and then (as the poet Michael Marra said) "gang hame tae their tea"? That horrible possibility might stop me voting Yes in the coming referendum. But I see hope in a Scots Labour MP speaking out against measures taken by a Scottish Nationalist Minister of Justice. My hope is that many Nationalist MPs will agree with him, so that the Scots parliament does *not* become a copy of the Westminster two-party system, in which for three centuries the Opposition spoke out for parliamentary reforms which it abandoned on taking office. This has been called *government by consensus*, and amounted to government by the richest. Local government by town and district councils was instituted at the end of the 19th century, and though elected councillors were often Tory, Liberal and Labour Party members, they did not divide along the party lines governing Westminster. Through them the greatest industrial cities in Scotland and England got what Glasgow had until the Thatcher era: their own good quality water, transport, lighting, healthcare, education and housing services, largely got because councillors of every persuasion recognized the good of it. When Mrs Thatcher used her parliamentary majority to strip trade unions and local councils of their powers, declaring it would establish democracy, the democracy she believed in was the power of her increasingly centralized London government.

I will vote Yes in the coming referendum in the faith and hope that we get a parliament whose main consensus will return power to its localities, and employ the police and health workers to defend and care for those without the means of folk in professional employment. Only in that way will we get a Scottish government which both trusts most people here and is trusted by them. What has happened to a land where the biggest city's local government decides to spend millions replacing thousands of surveillance cameras in its streets and public buildings? So Glasgow's police will soon have cameras that record what people *say*, as well as what they do. Under the new, extended laws people are likely to be arrested by the police on evidence supplied from police surveillance records. More widely shared knowledge of the present Scottish state, and intense public discussion of it, is needed to undo damage done to our homeland by a government that, like those of England and the USA, is out to increase control of everyone but the wealthiest, and do so on behalf of the wealthiest.

A journalist (I will not name her or him because authors should protect their sources) recently asked me if I would enter politics. I replied that a semi-alcoholic, octogenarian invalid was not the kind of politician Scotland needed. We need politicians below the age of forty-five with imaginative, independent minds, brave thinkers able to sit through boring meetings while staying alert. I was raving thirty years ago about the Scottish Labour Party's abandonment of Socialism to someone in it who said, "You are the kind of person our party needs! Join us!" I asked for advice from Archie Hind, one of my best friends and author of a great Glasgow novel, for he had always been a steady member of his local Labour Party. He advised me not to join, saying I could not stand the boredom. It was essential, he said, to hear a lot of useless talking before you could get a meeting to vote for or against something important. In those days he stopped one wealthy employer joining the Glasgow Labour Party under the rule that every owner of a business must ensure that their employees belong to a trade union. Tony Blair abolished that rule so Archie Hind abandoned the Labour Party. I am too impatient to be a useful member of any political party.

11: Letter to the Unknown Soldier

YOUR STATUE IN LONDON'S PADDINGTON STATION shows you in the uniform of a British soldier, so you may have been one of the English, Welsh, Irish and Scots soldiers who fought and died in the Great War. If so, I feel for you because my father may have fought beside you. He survived with a small shrapnel wound which required him to wear a truss for the rest of his life, and brought him a small pension from the British government which I now realize allowed me to be one of the British upper working classes – a privileged child born in one of the first housing estates built under the Wheatley Housing Act. He never spoke about his war experiences before my twenty-first birthday, when he mentioned he had returned to the front line in Flanders after leave at home. He said that as he advanced it became obvious that more British soldiers were retreating than advancing, and suddenly a bullet from a German sniper grazed his finger. At this he laughed and told a comrade, "That is the best birthday present I could ever have had! It will give me another fortnight of leave behind the front line." Like schoolfriends whose parents had also survived that war I was not interested in it, although later I had a friend whose father had been in World War II and boasted about all the Germans he had killed. But my son was fascinated to hear that his granddad had been part of the hideous 1914–18 slaughter. After seeing the film *Oh What a Lovely War* I suggested they watch it together. My dad said he thought it mainly accurate, except in its presentation of the 1914 Christmas Day armistice, when the big guns stopped shelling the front lines, and the British and German troops fraternized in what was called No Man's Land. The film suggested that the British officers accepted this. My dad said the ones he knew were enraged, brandishing their pistols and shouting, "Back to your trenches, you traitors!"

He said, "We turned our backs to them and there was nothing they could do. But on all the Christmases that happened afterwards the big guns on each side never stopped shelling."

So I am old enough to sympathize with those who fought in that war, whether British, German, French, Russian, Austrian, Italian or of any other nation driven into massacring each other in a way nobody had imagined or anticipated. A year or two after it began, the British Prime Minister told the editor of the *Guardian* that the British people must not be told the truth about the conditions of troops fighting in France, because if it was widely known the war would have to stop. The only end which both sides insisted upon was Unconditional Surrender, an outcome first insisted upon in the American Civil War of 1861 to 1865. Before that, even in the wars with Napoleon's European empire, it was assumed that the folk Napoleon commanded were obeying superior officers as their opponents did, so the French people were not to blame.

To keep our soldiers fighting in France the British government and its press announced that we were fighting to make *A Land Fit For Heroes To Live In*, and that the German people would be forced to pay for it. The result of our victory was that rich Germans who had led their nation into the war remained wealthy, while common Germans who obeyed them were brought to a level of starvation that had clerical workers stealing turnips from fields near their cities. Out of this financial catastrophe the Nazi Party was born. In Great Britain the seizing of German coal and other resources resulted in unemployment for British miners. The idiocy of this punitive foreign policy was publicized at the time by John Maynard Keynes, who is now regarded as the architect of the British Welfare State that existed after World War II created it. But you, who may have been a comrade of my father, did not survive long enough to see that.

The thought of those who died in World War I sometimes brings me to tears, though their names on memorial statues in every British parish have been added to by the names of those who died in World War II, and perhaps Tony Blair's later wars. Cairndhu on the shore of Loch Fyne lost over twenty of its men in World War I, to which roughly ten names were added to the lochside memorial after our second World War had indeed made life better for many of the working classes in Britain. In 1981 I was a guest of the Cairndhu schoolmistress, and we went to the open-air Armistice Day service of remembrance by that monument close to her home. It was conducted by the local minister who read words used in the English remembrance service: "They shall not grow old as we that are left grow old. At the going down of the sun we will remember them." This, with a bagpiper playing a coronach beside grey waters under a grey sky, moved me although the dead men named on the monument had been fooled into thinking they were fighting for a better Britain, while those who had died in World War II had certainly fought a wicked system of government. Next year my friend told me she could not bring herself to attend the remembrance service, which was now swamped by rejoicing over the British defeat of Argentina in the Falklands War, described by an American writer as "two bald men fighting over a comb".

I hate to say that, like my father, you were duped by publicity that the Britain you were defending would become a land fit for heroes to live in. I cannot say it was a pity that you did not live long enough, like my dad, to see it was a lie. But nowadays your sacrifice (as they now call it) is politically useful. Alex Salmond's Scottish government has arranged a referendum in September 2014, exactly six centuries after the Battle of Bannockburn which once achieved Scottish independence. Cameron's Westminster government has responded with the ploy of making 2014 a year of celebration for the outbreak of World War I! I am sure every nation involved in that war has celebrated its ending. I am sure the government of the United Kingdom is the only one to celebrate its beginning, but for a while Glasgow's Labour Council originally planned to join the celebrations. It would remove from

George Square the statues of Robert Burns, Walter Scott, James Watt, David Livingstone, Gladstone, perhaps even the equestrian statues of Queen Victoria and Prince Albert, leaving only the cenotaph before the City Chambers. This commemorates the two world wars, and an inscription says that in the first of them:

Total of His Majesty's forces engaged at home and abroad.

8654465

of this number the City of Glasgow raised over

200000

A scandal too dreary to recount here put the chief proponent of the statue removal scheme out of office and it was dropped. If carried through it would have made a wonderful space for military parades honouring not only the many who died to give us victories in the two world wars, but those who have fought abroad in many smaller wars since, including four as an ally of the USA. It may even have won some votes for the *Better Together* referendum campaign. That seems unlikely, but why else should the British government wish to celebrate the start of a war of which every nation that took part should be ashamed? So almost a century after your death politicians still have a use for it.

Postscript:
Talking Utopian

WHEN COMPLETING A BOOK IN RECENT YEARS, I realize that now I could make it a much better one if I started again and took more time. I cannot start again with this book if it is to be part of conversations before the September 2014 referendum. This last chapter will end messily with suggestions which should have each been a chapter in itself.

Think of good things enjoyed by other nations, some with fewer people than Scotland. The Netherlands have over three times our population, but that well-cultivated, partly submarine kingdom has so good a national health service that even the wealthy know they will not get better treatment by privately paying for it. Germany has now about eighty-two million people, almost a quarter more than those in our United Kingdom, but before unification a West German friend told me that where he came from only the rich parents of mentally impaired children paid to give them a special education: normal children of the rich would not get a better education than in the common state schools. What was, and I think still is, good healthcare and education in the Netherlands and Germany still exists in six Scandinavian nations, half of which are monarchies, though their royal families are not like ours. Their children go to the common state schools or have jobs in offices before assuming the throne. The king or queen can go shopping without being mobbed. How *strange* these foreigners are!

It is easy for governments to spend taxpayers' money on healthcare and education where every citizen is not taxed to pay for big armed forces and nuclear weapon bases, like the UK, the USA and China. Israel's population of over five million is as large as Scotland's, and also has nuclear weapons, but this cannot be discussed without bringing a charge of anti-Semitism, so I should not have mentioned it. But if Scotland could tax its offshore oil companies as Shetland does, and people here were not taxed to keep military forces and nuclear weapons which most of the world's nations do not have (partly because Britain and the USA would declare war on them if they were suspected of it), then a Scottish government chosen by folk living here could make this a more decent country.

Switzerland has no coastline, but is so sub-divided by mountains that its internal diversity resembles Scotland. It has four different national languages, a great part of it once adopted the Calvinist religion, and another part is Roman Catholic. In some ways it is the most democratic of modern nations, being ruled by perpetual referendums. Each canton or voting district has a perpetual polling booth where citizens can vote for or against acts being discussed in Bern, seat of the Swiss parliament. Swiss women were denied the vote before 1951 because it was said that good ones were too busy with housework and their children to bother with politics and voting. I only suggest Scotland adopt the Swiss practice of everyone expecting to know what their government is doing and being able to influence it more often than once every five years. The Chartists were a democratic movement of labourers, tradesmen and professional folk who tried to get parliamentary reform between 1838 and 1848. One of their demands was for a new parliamentary election every year, but after the Reform Bill gave the vote to most of the wealthy middle class this demand was found inconvenient. The UK, the USA and other nations who think themselves democratic are now mostly content with governments whose minds the voters can only change by a general election every five years unless they run riot. This happened in England over the poll tax, and in the USA over segregation and, to a lesser extent, over the Vietnam War. The Swiss perpetual referendum idea is a safer idea. The voting station could also be the local district councillor and member of parliament's local surgery. The building should be rent free to the users and a secretarial staff's salary paid by the taxpayer, though when councillors and members changed through an election they should be allowed to give these jobs to friends or relations.

Here is another Utopian idea not in use nowadays, though once it was taken for granted. With modern means of communication it could be easily practised in Scotland. When kings were the highest judges in every land, the government had to be wherever the king lived, so the Scottish capital kept shifting between Edinburgh, Linlithgow, Falkland, Stirling and Perth. Scottish kings were Lowlanders so did not risk taking the capital as far north as Inverness, the former Pictish kings' main seat of government. With the help of modern smartphones there is no reason why the Scottish parliament should not sometimes convene in any town with a railway station. It would be inconvenient for Lowland MPs to assemble at Inverness once in a while, but no more than for Highlands and Islands MPs to meet in Edinburgh. Our parliaments should convene especially in places most directly to be affected by their enactments. Since 1707 the curse of Scotland has been the fact that our MPs and lords have met in the Palace of Westminster. I was told by Norman Buchan, once a true Socialist, "As soon as you get to London and enter the House of Commons you see Scotland from a completely different perspective." We first met when campaigning in Dunoon against Holy Loch becoming an American nuclear weapons base. Later, as the Labour Party's Shadow Secretary of State for Scotland, he was totally opposed to the Scottish independence that in 1892 had been one of the Labour Party's aims.

The problem of every nation is being governed by folk with a *completely different perspective* – a different view of life – from those who elect them. This superior attitude is an occupational hazard or disease of any people with more power than most of us. It let Baroness Thatcher when a mere prime minister say, "It is my job to make life difficult for these people," when speaking of folk who mainly live in transport vehicles and had come together for a festival at Glastonbury. No politician should feel secure enough to talk like that about a minority, whether the minority is Gypsy, Jewish, Wee Free or even criminal. It is the job of the police to make life hard for criminals. I believe they do their best without politicians pressing them to be harder.

It should be the aim of every elected government to make life better for all those in their land, even those who have not elected them. If you disagree I will defend to the death your right to say so. But before these sensible, Utopian ideas are discussed it is essential that the Scottish legal system retrieves some independence it lost under the present Cabinet Secretary for Justice, Kenny MacAskill. This is especially true of the Scottish requirement of corroboration in criminal cases. MacAskill, defying the opinion of most Scottish judges, has tried to abolish that and bring it in line with its abolition in England. I once suspected this was part of an English takeover plot. I no longer believe this. I am sure England's bosses care very little about what the Scots do in their northern province, as long as they leave their natural resources in the hands of the main global enterprises. I believe MacAskill's mindset, like that of too many Scots in authority, assumes that what the richest English do is best, because he and others like him have a colonial attitude toward London, even when they are part of a *devolved* government. Our other need is to get an independent parliament whose members do not believe that civil security can be got by steadily increasing the powers of the police. In my Scots Anglo-Centralizing chapter I mentioned that the Scottish Fiscal Service had once been proudly independent of the police force, because its job was to judge police prosecutions impartially. But now the Fiscal Service is partly staffed by both serving and retired police officers, so impartiality is to that extent reduced. It should be brought back. Like most other nations, Scotland should have a written constitution. The United States was established with a fairly good one, though more and more amendments have been made to it. Britain's United Kingdom is famous for having none, which allows any long-lasting parliamentary majority to do what it likes. Most states that were once part of the USSR Empire had written constitutions, with clauses to guarantee democratic opposition which their governments ignored. It is now forgotten that the main opposers who brought down the East German Republic were not enthusiasts for Capitalist governments, but Socialists who objected to a single-party dictatorship. The Republic of Ireland has a constitution which declares its government must be neutral – meaning take no side – in conflicts between other governments. Between 2001 and 2005 it became known Shannon airport was being used by the United States for *extraordinary rendition* – the transport of captured people suspected of terrorism to jails where they could be held without trial and tortured. Because this violated the Irish Republic's constitutional neutrality, some Irish broke into and damaged a USA aircraft, and were arrested for this. Before the case was tried in an Irish court, ex-President Carter announced that he would appear as a witness for the defence, as he thought extraordinary rendition was in itself a crime. So the matter was never brought to court. I wish Scotland would get a constitution asserting its neutrality.

And finally let me give you THE DECLARATION OF CALTON HILL which appears in another book of mine but which should be relevant here. When Queen Elizabeth the First of the whole United Kingdom opened Scotland's new parliament building in 2004, the Scottish Socialist Party held a counter-demonstration on Calton Hill. The SSP made up a minority of the demonstrators. Most of those present only agreed that a lady entitled to an Imperial Crown was not needed to authorize a people's parliament. I was flattered and excited when Mr Sheridan said his party was planning a Declaration of Intent for Scotland, and suggested I and James Kelman draft it. We did. The Scottish Socialist Party (God rest its innocent soul) did not use much of what we wrote. Here it is.

*We, the Undersigned, want a Scottish Commonwealth
where people of every origin, trade, profession and faith
work for each other's welfare.*

*We believe this State needs a parliament elected by Scotland's
people, and recognizing these people as its only sovereign.
We believe this parliament's members and agencies should
be the servants, not masters, of Scotland's people, through
a written constitution that promises everyone the right to
freely vote, speak and assemble; the right to protection
from injury, theft and invasion of privacy; the right to know
all the doings of its government and its agencies, with all
the sources of its members' income, since a public servant's
income is the business of the public. We believe that under
this constitution, Scotland's parliament should completely
control Scotland's revenues, and use them –*

1. To negotiate as an equal with other governments.
*2. To defend the health, property and safety of life in
Scotland by limiting or acquiring land or properties within
Scottish borders that are owned by outside corporations or
government agencies.*
*3. To work to make public housing, transport, education,
legal aid and healthcare as good as any purchasable by
private wealth.*

*None of these three requirements has priority.
We do not want an independent Scotland because we
dislike the English, but because we want separation
from that Union of financial, military and monarchic
establishments calling itself Great Britain.*

Goodbye